A lecturer once told me,

"How do you always know the colour of your front door? It's because you've see it every day."

This book works in a similar fashion, you need to read over these notes as much as possible and soon enough it will become second nature to you. The same goes with clinical practice, the more you see patients with the same presentations the more you'll know what to look for each time and how to manage them.

Test yourself:

When you feel confident enough, test yourself by trying to write out these notes from memory. Use the contents page to write out all the conditions in this book. With the eyes, ears and skin sections of this book, cover the coloured half of the pages to test yourself and see if you can work out the diagnosis from the image.

	Page		Page
GENERAL MEDICINE		Rectal exam	36
Diabetes	6	Benign prostatic hyperplasia	36
Thyroid disorders	9	UTI	36
Adrenal disorders	10	Urinary retention	37
Myocardial Infarction	11	Urinary incontinence	37
Angina & N/STEMI	11	Erectile dysfunction	38
Hypertension	12	Scrotal swelling & pain	38
Hypertension review	13	Haematuria	38
Valves & murmurs	13	Blood in the stool	39
Neutropenia	14	Bowel cancer	39
Sepsis	14	Glomerular nephropathies	39
ECG's	14	Nephrotic syndrome	40
ABG's	15	Nephritic syndrome	41
Types of pacemaker	16	Acute kidney injury	42
Atrial fibrillation	16	Chronic kidney disease	43
Heart failure	17	Clostridium difficile	43
Pericardial effusions	19	MRSA	44
Pneumonia	19	Antimicrobials	44
Fibrosis	21	Side effects of cardiac drugs	45
Pneumothorax	21	OBSTETRICS & GYNAE	
Bronchiectasis	22	Measuring the pregnancy	47
Asthma	23	Dietary supplements	47
COPD	25	Gestational diabetes	47
Lung function	26	Fits during pregnancy	48
Anaphylaxis	26	Hypertension	48
Emphysema	27	Pre-eclampsia	49
Tuberculosis	27	Anaemia	49
Peptic ulcer disease	28	Thrombocytopenia	50
Oesophageal varices	28	Von willbrands	50
Inflammatory bowel	29	Sickle cell anaemia	50
Diverticulitis	30	DVT to PE	51
Liver disease	31	UTI	51
Liver function tests	32	Placental abruption	52
Appendicitis	32	Placenta praevia	52
Small bowel obstruction	33	Postpartum haemorrhage	53
Ischaemic bowel	34	Inducing labour	53
Pancreatitis	34	Cardiotocograph	53
Inguinal hernias	35	Cord prolapse	54
Anal cancer	35	Foetal bradycardia	54
Anal pain	35	Shoulder dystocia	54

Thrush	55	Myasthenia gravis	75
Bacterial vaginosis	55	Multiple sclerosis	76
Trichomonas vaginalis	56	Strokes	77
Chlamydia trachomatis	56	Epilepsy	77
Gonorrhea	57	Focal limb weakness	79
Pelvic inflammatory disease	57	Syncope causes	79
Dysmenorrhagia	58	Mental health law	80
Fibroids	58	GP: Diarrhoea	81
Endometriosis	58	GP: Constipation	81
Polycystic ovaries	59	GP: Vomiting	82
Tumour markers	59	GP: Headaches	82
Ovarian cyst accidents	60	GP: Back pain	84
Contraception	60	GP: Muscle pain	84
Abortion and miscarriage	61	Elderly patients	85
Mastitis	62	Paed: UTI	86
Nipple thrush	62	Paed: Balanitis	86
Breast cancer	63	Paed: Hypospadias	87
Postpartum blues	63	Paed: Noctural enuresis	87
GP AND MENTAL HEALTH		Paed: Haemolytic-uraemic syndrome	87
Parkinson's	65	Paed: Acid reflux	88
Essential tremor	66	Paed: Bronchiolitis	88
Dementia	66	Paed: URTI	89
Parkinson plus conditions	66	Paed: Epiglottitis	89
Acute stress reaction	67	Paed: Croup	90
Adjustment disorder	67	Paed: pertussis	90
Depression	68	Paed: Tonsillitis	91
Bipolar	68	Paed: Blood pressure	92
Mania	69	Paed: Diabetes	92
Schizophrenia	69	Paed: Hypothyroid	94
Anxiety	70	Paed: Mesenteric adenitis	95
Panic attack	70	OPHTHALMOLOGY	
Delirium	71	Ophthalmic history	97
Personality disorder	71	Ocular motion	98
Obsessive compulsive disorder	72	Anisocoria	98
Autism	72	Afferent pupillary defect	99
ADHD	73	Adies	99
Suicide	73	Horner's	99
Neuromuscular disorders	74	Visual fields	100
Guillian barre	74	Ophthalmoscopes	101
Motor neuron disease	75	Blepharitis	103

Conjunctivitis	104	Plaster removal	147
Corneal abrasion	105	Air in the abdomen	148
Keratitis	105	DERMATOLOGY	
Pterygium	105	Basal Cell carcinomas	
Chalazion	106	Squamous Cell carcinomas	
Dacrocytitis	106	Bowens	
Ectropion	107	Melanoma	
Entropion	107	Uticaria	
Glaucoma	107	Angioedema	
Blow out fracture	108	Erythema Nodosum	
Thyroid eye disease	109	Erythema Multiforme	
Subconjunctival haemorrhage	109	Steven Johnson Syndrome	
Hyphema	109	Erythroderma	
Iritis	110	Discoid Eczema	
Gonococcal/Chlamydia	110	Pampholyx eczema	
EARS		Impetigo	
Example otoscopes	113	Eczema herpeticum	
NOSE & THROAT		Pityriasis versicolour	
Rhinitis	122	Vitiligo	
Chronic rhinitis	123	Xanthoma	
Nose bleeds	123	Psoriasis	
Haemorrhagic telangiectasia	124	Plaque psoriasis	
Juvenile haemangiofibroma	124	Lichinification	
Maxillofacial pain	125	Keloid scar	
Stridor	125	Acne	
Thyroglossal duct cyst	126	Shingles	
OVERDOSE & ELECTOLYTE DISORDER		HSV1 & HSV2	
Drug overdoses	128	Chicken pox	
Electrolyte imbalances	131	Molloscum contagiosum	
Primary survey	135	Hand, foot and mouth	
ORTHOPAEDICS		Erythema infectiosum	
Osteoporosis	140	Pityriasis rosea	
Osteoarthritis	140	Intertrigo	
Chest x-ray	141	Erysipelas	
Abdominal x-ray	142	Folliculitis	
Hip fractures	143	Quick differentials	165
Wrist fractures	145	Spotting a sick child	168
Ankle fractures	146	PRACTISE QUESTIONS	
Compartment syndrome	146	Quiz	171
Septic arthritis	147	Answers	173

Scenario questions	178	Practice ECG's	187
Scenario answers	186	Practice ABG's	201

The pancreas is split into two parts, exocrine and endocrine. For diabetes we are concerned with the endocrine function.

The exocrine pancreas secretes trypsin, chymotrypsin and bicarbonate (HCO_3^-) into the duodenum. This part of the pancreas constitutes 95% of the overall pancreas. It includes:

- Acinar and ducts cells

The endocrine pancreas secretes glucagon (Alpha cells), insulin (Beta cells), somatostatin (Delta cells) and pancreatic polypeptide (Gamma cells).

Diabetic symptoms:

- Polyuria
- Weight loss
- Lethargy
- Dizziness
- Blurred vision
- Retinopathy
- Neuropathy
- Thirstiness
- Ketonuria
- Glucosuria
- Foot ulcers
- Peripheral vascular disease

Diabetes type 1(DM1) = Autoimmune disorder of T-cells causing the destruction of beta cells. This lack of insulin producing cells leads to insulin deficiency which causes hyperglycaemia. Without treatment patients can develop diabetic ketoacidosis (DKA) which can progress to a coma and death.

Diabetic ketoacidosis occurs due to the lack of insulin, this prevents the body from absorbing glucose. Therefore, the liver compensates by breaking down fats into ketones for energy. Ketones are acidic and dehydrate the patient, therefore DKA needs to be treated with fluid resuscitation.

Diabetes type 2 (DM2) = Age related resistance to insulin. Insulin cannot correctly enter cells because body cells are not as sensitive to it so the pancreas initially compensates by increasing insulin production. However, the pancreas cannot cope and beta cells soon fail. Patients are usually over the age of 55yrs and are obese or overweight. Therefore, first line of treatment is always exercise and dietary changes.

Treatment

- Insulin
- Potassium
- Bicarbonate
- IV Saline
- Statin to reduce the cardiovascular risk (not for pregnant women (teratogenic))

Diabetic medication:

Sulfonylureas e.g. *Gliclazide* (can cause Hypoglycaemia)

Thiazolidinediones increases insulin sensitisation (used in DM2) but has a risk of bladder cancer and osteoporosis

Glucophage e.g. *Metformin* increases insulin sensitisation. Side effects include diarrhoea. It is important to avoid the use of *Metformin* with poor renal function, contrast mediums for CT, or heart failure because it can cause lactic acidosis.

DPP-IV blocks the enzyme which breaks down GLP-1

Injections:

Very Fast acting insulin e.g. *Novorapid/HuminsulinS*

Long acting insulin e.g. *Glargine/Huminsulinl*

Combination (biphasic) insulin e.g. *Novomix*

Insulin pump therapy aims to more closely mimic the function of a healthy pancreas. The pump uses fast acting insulin such as *Novorapid*. It involves having a small cannula placed in the subcutaneous fat, usually around the waist. This is connected to the insulin pump which provides the insulin infusion boluses.

GLP is a hormone produce by intestinal cells when exposed to carbohydrate. **GLP1** analogues imitate the effects of GLP1 but with a longer half-life. It causes insulin secretion, inhibition of glucagon and decreased insulin resistance. It also reduces gastric emptying and therefore causes satiety and weight loss. Sadly this drug is expensive and has a risk of causing pancreatitis. Therefore it is only given for patients with poor control and obesity.

Lipohypertrophy is a medical term that refers to a lump under the skin caused by the accumulation of extra fat at the site of many subcutaneous insulin injections. It can be a cause of hypoglycaemia.

HBA1C: By measuring the levels of glycosylated haemoglobin it can measure the levels of glucose in the blood over the last 3-4 months (average lifespan of a red blood cell). Also used in the diagnosis of DM2.

Plasma glucose level: <6 mmol/L is a healthy fasting level glucose.

6-7mmol/L is pre diabetes/impaired fasting.

>7mmol/L retinopathy tends to begin.

Glucose tolerance test: Fasting overnight + 75g glucose drink + glucose in 2hrs. If:

<11mmol/L (healthy)

7-11mmol/L (impaired)

>11 (DM1 or DM2).

Gestational diabetes: fasting glucose of >5.6mmol/L. Glucose tolerance of >7.8mmol/L.

Management

Annual review of: retinopathy and neuropathy

Quality of life, smoking, BP, activity.

With diabetes you should also check thyroid function for any autoimmune attacks of the thyroid as well as coeliac disease which are both more common in diabetics.

Other causes of diabetes

Dispogenic = A defect to the hypothalamus causing malfunction of the thirst mechanism. Patients will consume large volumes of fluid supressing vasopressin and increasing their urine output.

Gestational = During pregnancy the placenta produces vasopressinase which breaks down vasopressin. Gestational diabetes is believed to be an overproduction of vasopressinase.

Diabetes Insipidus = Characterised by the passage of large volumes of dilute urine. It can rapidly cause dehydration leading to death if it is not appropriately managed.

THYROID DISORDERS

Imbalanced production of thyroid hormones arises from the dysfunction of either the thyroid gland, the pituitary gland, which produces thyroid-stimulating hormone (TSH), or the hypothalamus, which regulates the pituitary gland via thyrotropin-releasing hormone (TRH). Concentrations of TSH increase with age, requiring age-corrected tests.

Hypothyroidism = Autoimmune	Hyperthyroidism = Excess Thyroid hormone
E.g. Hashimoto's Symptoms: • Weight gain • Slowed heart rate • Constipation • Heavy irregular periods • Joint and muscle pain • Cold sensitivity • Fatigue Treatment *Levothyroxine / Triiodothyronine /* Desiccated thyroid extract	E.g. Grave's Disease Symptoms: • Weight loss • Fast heart rate • Diarrhoea • Retracted eyelids • Exophthalmos • Muscle pain • Enlarged thyroid Treatment Radioiodine / Anti-thyroid drugs (*Carbimazole*) / Surgically remove and provide hormone replacement tablets
Severe state = Myxoedema Coma Treatment: Thyroxine	Severe state = Thyrotoxicosis Treatment: Beta blocker, *Carbimazole* and *Propylthiouracil*

SYNACTHEN TEST is used to assess the adrenals

Addison's < Glucocorticoid	Cushing's >Cortisol	Conns >Aldosterone
• Hypercalcaemia • Hyperpigmentation (Nipple, cheek, skin creases) • Joint and muscle pain • Metabolic Acidosis Due to the low aldosterone you also get • Hyperkalaemia • Hyponatremia Treatment hydrocortisone tablets/ prednisone tablets	• Weight gain • Red face • Moon face • Excess hair growth (women) • Extra fat around neck • Poor concentration and memory • Hump on back Treatment Surgical excision followed by hormonal replacement such as steroids because of risk of adrenal crisis.	• Hypernatremia • Hypokalaemia • Metabolic alkalosis • Tingling sensation (paraesthesia) • Muscle weakness • Headaches • Excess urination Treatment Surgical removal for a benign tumour Spironolactone for Hyperplasia of the adrenal gland

Adrenal Crisis: Anyone on 10 or more days of steroids needs to be tapered off to avoid adrenal crisis. Also check to see if they are on anti-fungal medication as this can sometimes cause an adrenal crisis. Symptoms are hypotension or shock. Give adrenocorticotropic hormone (ACTH) and test to see if there is any response, if there is not then treat with hydrocortisone (100mg) and fluids.

Pheochromocytoma: A tumour of the adrenal gland causing a high blood pressure with elevated levels of adrenaline, noradrenaline, and increased cardiac output. Usually this will present in young people with poor blood pressure control, palpitations, anxiety and intermittent attacks. Test with 24 hour urine monitoring for catecholamines. Treat first with an alpha antagonist and then a beta antagonist.

When blood flow stops reaching a part of the heart it causes damage to the heart muscle. The most common symptom is chest pain or discomfort which may travel into the shoulder, arm, back, neck, or jaw due to irritation of the phrenic nerve. Often it is in the centre or left side of the chest and lasts for more than a few minutes. The mechanism often involves the complete blockage of a coronary artery caused by a rupture of an atherosclerotic plaque which is very prothrombotic. Infarction (dead tissue) produces an abnormal ECG discussed later in this book.

- Troponin is a heart muscle protein that can be measured in the blood (this will be elevated at 2 hours following an MI and will be at its highest at around 6 hours)

In an emergency setting

Use this acronym "CAN I/ME SOB?"

Clopidogrel, **A**spirin, **N**itrate, **I**V heparin, **M**orphine, anti-**E**metic, **S**tatin, **O**pioid, **B**eta blocker

A proton pump inhibitor (PPI) should be given with any blood thinners to prevent gastric bleeds.

Dressler's Syndrome is the development of pericarditis (inflammation in the pericardial sac) which can sometimes take place several weeks after a myocardial infarction. Like other forms of pericarditis, it can present with chest pain, difficulty breathing, and fever.

ANGINA , NSTEMI & STEMI

An atherosclerotic plaque that has a smooth, regular surface which means that it can block a certain amount of blood flow. This is fine in normal circumstances but when you exert yourself blood flow does not adequately meet your oxygen requirements and you end up with sore heart muscle, known as angina.

Stable angina is the form of angina that does not occur at rest. Rather, it comes on after a certain amount of exertion so is therefore quite predictable.

Unstable angina is where the plaque is irregular, or partially ruptured, this exposes the inner plaque which is very prothrombotic and a clot forms over this area, further occluding the coronary vessel. You will now have chest pain even at rest. If this chest pain happens to be related to some muscle ischaemia leading to some myonecrosis, you'll get the release of troponin from the cardiac muscle cells. When this happens, you've got yourself a Non-ST segment elevation myocardial Infarction (**NSTEMI**) which cannot be treated with thrombolytics. Instead treat with 'CAN I/ME SOB'. If severe it can be useful to use the GRACE score to assess their severity and if they require an angiogram.

ST segment elevation myocardial infarction **(STEMI),** happens when you have an infarction that causes full thickness muscle death at some place in the heart. It is usually caused by a blood clot getting caught in a plaqued artery. Since this section of muscle is now dead and not electrically active, you get a change in the ECG which just happens to now show the electrical activity on the opposite wall which is still alive. As the cause is a clot it can be treated with thrombolytics or cardiac catheterisation.

HYPERTENSION

Hypertension refers to persistently raised blood pressure above 140/90mmHg. **Essential hypertension** is the most common reason and has an unknown cause. Ambulatory blood pressure monitoring should be done for patients with new high blood pressure before trialling medication.

<55 years old
- ACEi (Angiotensin converting enzyme inhibitor) e.g. *Ramipril* (side effect of dry cough)
- ARB (Angiotensin 2 receptor blockers) e.g. *Losartan*

[Both drugs are teratogenic therefore should not be used in pregnant women]

>55 years old / black ethnicity
- CCB (Calcium channel blockers) e.g. *Amlodipine* (side effects of swollen ankles, rash)
- TLD (Thiazide like diuretic) e.g. *Indapamide* (use if patient also has heart failure)

If BP remains high
- CCB + ACEi/ARB........CCB + ACEi/ARB + TLD........CCB + ACEi/ARB + TLD + alpha/beta blocker (side effect of male impotence)

Secondary hypertension = An underlying secondary cause:

- Renal disease (Pyelonephritis, Renal artery stenosis)
- Endocrine disease (Cushing's, Acromegaly, Hyperparathyroidism, Pheochromocytoma)
- Pregnancy, Steroids, Drugs
- Cardiac (Coarctation of aorta)
- Vascular (Polyarteritis nodosa, Lupus(SLE))

Malignant hypertension = Malignant hypertension is a syndrome characterised by severely elevated blood pressure accompanied by retinopathy (retinal haemorrhages, exudates or papilloedema), nephropathy (malignant nephrosclerosis) with or without encephalopathy and anaemia. It is usually a consequence of untreated essential or secondary hypertension. Renal function should be monitored daily, as the initial BP reduction is often associated with deterioration in renal function.

Beta blocker/ CCB / IV Sodium Nitroprusside if no oral therapy can be administered. The initial aim of treatment is to lower blood pressure in a rapid (within 2-6 hours) but controlled way.

HYPERTENSION REVIEWS

Ask about any complaints, their treatment, how it's taken, how many tablets are left, was it taken today, and any side effects. Then ask:

- Exercise, salt/animal fat, smoking or alcohol, stress
- Previous BP, headaches/dizziness
- Cough, Chest pain, TIA (Vision loss, CVA),
- Last ECG/Bloods/X-Ray
- Co-morbidities
- Last period, are they planning a baby, contraception, condoms
- Ideas, Concerns and Expectations

MURMURS & VALVES

Diastolic murmurs = These murmurs are heard on the second heart sound

- Aortic regurgitation (lean patient forward and listen at pulmonary area with diaphragm of stethoscope)
- Mitral stenosis (causes malar flush)(can be caused by rheumatic fever)

Systolic murmurs = These murmurs are heard on the first heart sound

- Aortic Stenosis (causes a louder S1 and soft S2)
- Mitral valve prolapse (click sound)
- Mitral regurgitation (mid systolic rumble) (lean patient left and listen with the bell of the stethoscope)
- Pulmonary stenosis (Splitting of S2)
- Ventricular septal defect
- Atrial septal defect

Aortic stenosis is very common and can arise from one of three conditions:

- Congenital
- Acquired e.g. rheumatic fever (Strep pyogenes autoantibodies target the heart, joints, skin and brain)
- Calcification of valves (damage to vessels causes calcium to deposit)

Murmurs are scaled 1-5 with 5 being loud enough to hear without a stethoscope!

Aortic dissection = Cut in the aortic walls, the tunica media gets weaker and blood enters between the tunica interna and tunica media, 'dissecting' a new route.

(Large pulse pressure = Aortic regurgitation) (Narrow pulse pressure = Aortic stenosis)

NEUTROPENIA

Causes:

- HIV
- Chemotherapy/Radiation
- Cancer
- Aplastic anaemia
- Pregnant

SEPSIS

Symptoms include: Low blood pressure and high/low heart rate, fever/cold, high respiratory rate

The 3 in, 3 out rule

-Give Fluids

-Give O_2 (15L Breather mask)

-Give antibiotics (IV antibiotic e.g. *Tazocin*)

-Get lactate

-Get blood culture

-Get urine culture

ECG

1st degree block = P-R interval extended (>5squares/>2ms)

2nd degree block = P-R interval gets longer and then a QRS is missed / P-R interval is fixed at a 1st degree block but will misses the occasional QRS

3rd degree block or complete heart block = No relation between P and QRS. Treatment for a 3rd degree block is *Atropine* and cardioversion. Patients will also need a lifelong implantable pacemaker. Bradycardia also treated with *Atropine*.

Wolf-Parkinson-White syndrome = A congenital abnormality with short PR-intervals, a wide QRS-complex with a delta wave. Treatment includes anti-arrhythmic drugs or ablation.

Sick sinus syndrome = Sinus bradycardia or sinus pauses. Treatment is a pacemaker.

VT= Patients will present with syncope and chest pain and may have had a long QT segment prior to this. VT can progress to VF/Torse de pointe. IV *sotalol* or *Amiodarone* is used to treat the patient if they are stable and have a monomorphic ECG form. Treatment for either VT or VF if in an unstable monomorphic ECG form is cardioversion. For an unstable polymorphic form defibrillation is used. Patients will need a life long pacemaker.

SVT= Can be asymptomatic with sinus tachycardia. If the patient is stable perform vasovagal manoeuvres such as rubbing the carotid artery. If unsuccessful use *Adenosine*. If this is also unsuccessful block the AV node with CCB/Beta blockers. In unstable patients cardioversion is used.

Atrial fibrillation = No P waves present

Right coronary artery affected = Atrial arrhythmia

Left coronary artery affected = Ventricular arrhythmia

Right Branch Bundle Block = M shape on leads v1-3

Left Branch Bundle Block = W shape on v1, M shape on v6 and AVF

Tri-fascicular block = 1st degree block + RBBB + Left axis deviation

Ischaemia = Inverted T waves

ARTERIAL BLOOD GAS

PCO$_2$ (4-6) DKA lowers PCO$_2$ from a high breathing rate (treat with fluid)

HCO$_3$- (25-30)

PO$_2$ (10.6-14.6) Can be low due to pneumonia

pH (7.35-7.45) Tricyclic antidepressant overdose lowers pH (treat with HCO$_3$-)

Single chamber = leads in right atria/right ventricle

Dual chamber = leads in right atria +right ventricle

Biventricular = right atria + right ventricle +left ventricle

ECG will have no P waves. It can be caused by: Old age, Hypertension-atrial dilation, Ischaemia, P.E, MI, Hyper/othyroidism

The production of clots can take place from stagnant blood in the atria, this should be prevented by making patients take anticoagulant. Evaluate with CHAD-2 score: Coronary heart disease, Hypertension, Age >75 years, DM1/DM2. In general, a score greater than 2 requires oral anticoagulation therapy, usually warfarin.

Treatment: **A**miodarone/ **B**eta blockers/ **C**ardioversion (if haemodynamically unstable) / **D**igoxin

Typically patients must be anticoagulated for many months, or have an atrial thrombus ruled out by echocardiogram before cardioversion is attempted for atrial fibrillations of unknown duration.

Surgical treatment: Ablation (cauterising abnormal electrical pathways) / Atrial appendage occlusion (prevents stagnant blood in the heart).

Holiday heart syndrome is characterized by the development of a tachyarrhythmia (often atrial fibrillation) in heavy drinkers after an episode of binging. Generally, this rhythm should resolve within 24 hours, so patients usually do not require any medications or surgery.

Chronic heart failure is defined as the inability of the heart to maintain adequate cardiac output and blood pressure to meet the body's requirements. Symptoms from Left Heart Failure (LHF) & Right Heart Failure (RHF) often overlap, so don't worry if you have a mixed picture. The most common cause of RHF is LHF, therefore patients often present with both. If both the left & right ventricles are affected this is known as Congestive heart failure (CHF). The ejection fraction of the heart normally should be = (50-70%) but is reduced in CHF.

Left ventricular failure	Right ventricular failure
• Dyspnoea • Fatigue • Orthopnoea • Cough – pink frothy sputum • Cold peripheries	• Peripheral oedema • Ascites • Nausea • Anorexia • Facial swelling
Left ventricular failure • Resting tachycardia • Systolic BP↓ • Tachypnoea • Crackles at lung base • Laterally displaced apex – Left Ventricle dilatation • Right ventricular heave – pulmonary hypertension	**Right ventricular failure** • Resting tachycardia • Systolic BP↓ • Pitting peripheral oedema • Nocturia • Ascites • Hepatomegaly • JVP↑

Hypertension commonly leads to left ventricular hypertrophy, which can progress to CHF. Antihypertensive therapy can sometimes reduce the progression of left ventricular hypertrophy.

Left ventricular hypertrophy causes myocardial ischemia because there is more muscle tissue which increases the demand for blood. Unfortunately there is also an insufficient capillary network in the thickened muscle which cannot supply all of it.

Elevated levels of brain natriuretic peptide (BNP) are also consistent with heart failure and is released from stretching of the heart muscle. The patient may experience prerenal acute kidney injury (AKI) due to renal hypoperfusion.

Chest X-ray

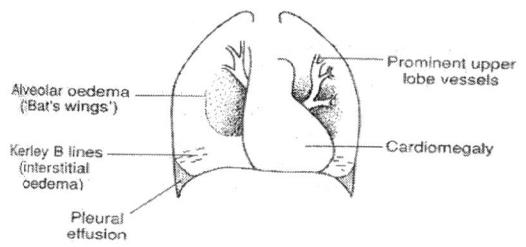

The CXR in left ventricular failure

Cardiomegaly is a cardiothoracic ratio greater than 50%. Patients with heart failure that experience a heart attack can have a sudden pleural effusion and may present breathless.

Drugs to avoid with heart failure:

-NSAIDs, *aspirin* or *ibuprofen*

-Calcium-channel blockers (CCB)

•Rate limiting non-dihydropyridine CCB e.g. *verapamil* and *diltiazem*

•First generation dihydropyridine derivatives e.g. *nifedipine*

-Tricyclic antidepressants (TCA)

-Lithium

-St John's wort (*hypericum perforatum*) (interacts with many drugs)

Treatment

Diuretics	Should be used to reduce cardiac congestion & fluid retention (*Furosemide*)
First line	ACE inhibitor + Beta Blocker *(Ramipril + Atenolol)*
Second line	All of the above + Aldosterone Antagonist (Spironolactone)/ Angiotensin Receptor Blocker (Losartan)/ Hydralazine + Nitrate *(*especially in people of African or Caribbean origin)
Third line	Cardiac Resynchronisation Therapy *(pacing with or without a defibrillator)* + Digoxin

Contraindications

Co-morbidity	
COPD/asthma/reversible airways disease	Beta-blockers are contra-indicated in patients with reversible airways disease
Renal dysfunction (serum creatinine > 200 µmol/l)	ACE inhibitors and angiotensin II receptor antagonists may be contraindicated
Anaemia	In anaemia due to heart failure, erythropoietin may improve symptoms and reduce risk of hospitalisation for worsening heart failure
Thyroid disease	Severe thyroid dysfunction may cause or precipitate heart failure
Peripheral vascular disease	High index of suspicion for renal artery stenosis required
Urinary frequency	Alpha blockers may cause hypotension or fluid retention but are not contraindicated
Gout	Avoid NSAIDs; gout may be exacerbated by diuretics

PERICARDIAL EFFUSIONS

Pericardial effusions can be caused by:

- malignancy.
- viral or infectious pericarditis
- autoimmune disease
- recent myocardial infarction

The classic signs on physical examination are hypotension, muffled heart sounds, and jugular venous distention. On ECG, pericardial effusion shows sinus tachycardia, small QRS complexes, and electrical alternans (an alternating QRS direction with each heartbeat, due to the swinging of the fluid surrounding the heart). In a patient who have symptom of pericardial effusion, an echocardiogram is the best test to establish a pericardial effusion.

Pericardial tamponade is when there is an accumulation of fluid within the pericardium. The increased fluid accumulation leads to pressure on the heart. This in turn decreases the stroke volume as the heart is unable to fill with blood. Suspect cardiac tamponade in any recent trauma to the chest such as in a car accident.

Community acquired pneumonia = infection of the lung usually by streptococcus in non-hospitalised patients causing fluid build-up in the alveoli. It can be diagnosed with a urine streptococcus test or sputum culture.

Symptoms:

- Shivers
- Pain
- Sweating
- Cough
- Tachypnoea
- Sputum

- Dull percussion over consolidation
- Cyanosis
- Reduced air entry (crackles)
- Use of accessory muscles

Patients are often managed by a CURB score: Confusion, Urea (>7), Respiratory rate (>30) and BP (<90/60). Each scores one point and results in the following next steps:

0-1: Treat as an outpatient

2: Short stay in hospital or as an outpatient

3-5: Hospitalization with consideration as to whether they need to be in the intensive care unit

Remember that pneumonia in immunocompromised/splenectomy patients can spread to meningitis. Therefore assess neurological function. If haemoptysis is present it is most likely an Aspergillosis infection.

Treatment

Drink plenty of fluids

Amoxicillin / Doxycycline/ Clarithromycin (penicillin allergy)

Ciprofloxacin for suspected Pseudomonas Aeruginosa

Atypical Pneumonia is a pneumonia not caused by the traditional pathogens and lacks many of the symptoms typically seen but can sometimes produce sputum. Chest x-rays often show the infection but often has poor response to common antibiotics.

This is fibrosis which takes place between the alveoli epithelium, capillary epithelium and the framework of lung tissue, giving restrictive ventilation.

Symptoms include inspiratory crackles, cor pulmonale, type 2 respiratory failure and erythema nodosum.

Causes:

- Churge-strausse
- Sjogren's
- Sarcoidosis
- Rheumatoid arthritis
- Drug (*amiodarone, methotrexate, aspirin*)
- Pneumonia
- COP (Cryptogenic organised pneumonia)

PNEUMOTHORAX

Bulla (cystic airspaces) or blebs (subpleural air spaces) can rupture and introduce air inside the pleural cavity and around the lungs. Pneumothorax - air in the thorax!

Symptoms include tachycardia/tachypnoea, low O_2 saturation, cyanosis, difficulty speaking, pallor, sweating and quiet breath sounds. Also check if the patient is haemodynamically unstable due to mediastinal shift by measuring blood pressure and pulse.

Once a pneumothorax is suspected, X-ray the chest to confirm the diagnosis, to assess the degree of any collapse (small <2cm around the lung or large >2cm), and to check for fluid levels.

Types of Pneumothorax:

- Smoker
- Lung disease   Secondary (Treat with chest drain insertion)
- Age >50years

- Haemodynamically unstable   Primary (Treat with aspiration)

<u>Emergency treatment</u>: Immediately aspirate at the mid-clavicular line 2nd-3rd intercostal space with a grey-needle (grade 14). This allows the air to escape out of the body.

<u>Surgical treatment</u>: includes pleuradhesis (reducing the space between pleural layers) or talcum powder (seals the pleural layers together)

<u>Observation and send home</u>: If the patient is haemodynamically stable with no pain or breathlessness and the pneumothorax is <2cm they can be observed without treatment.

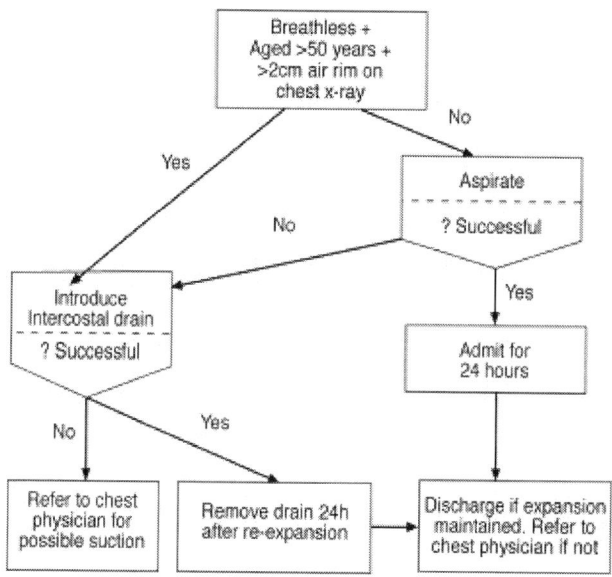

BRONCHIECTASIS

Bronchiectasis is the abnormal dilation of the major airways. Symptoms include recurrent chest infections, sputum production and haemoptysis. The most common cause of bronchiectasis is a history of chest infections. CT scans will show increased bronchial size with a characteristic 'signet ring' shape. Bronchiectasis in most cases is considered irreversible. Treatment of bronchiectasis is to try to decrease inflammation and infections. In patients with known bronchiectasis, infections should be treated promptly and aggressively to decrease the risk of further damage and dilatation of the airways.

Pleural effusion is fluid in the pleural space. This can be either exudative or transudative.

Exudates indicate that a local process is occurring, such as an infection so will have more protein in it (immunoglobulin (Ig)) whereas transudate wouldn't have as much protein. On X-ray, the lung looks like it's surrounded by whiteness with a meniscus shape. Also it can hide the breath sounds when listening to the chest.

Causes: Cancer, high blood pressure, TB, pneumonia, trauma, PE, lupus (SLE)

Pulmonary oedema occurs when the alveolar beds get engorged in the lungs. Compared to pleural effusion where there is a pool of fluid pushing on your lung, this time you have fluid inside your lung.

Causes: Fluid overload or cardiac failure. You either have too much fluid in your body and it ends up in your alveoli or your heart cannot pump the blood fast enough and pools fluid in your alveoli. On X-ray you would see congested lungs and someone with an enlarged heart. You can also see congestion of the great vessels, pulmonary congestion, where the peri-hilar area looks fluffy (the bat's wings sign) and Kerley B lines.

ASTHMA

Bronchospasm due to a gas exchange imbalance. Caused by:

- Stress (tachypnoeic)
- Infection (sputum can be green)
- Allergy

Causes a polyphonic wheeze from constricted bronchioles. The liver may be pushed down by the diaphragm (not enlarged) and heart sounds are quiet, both due to hyper-inflated lungs. Patients may state its worse when lying down or at "night time" but this may actually be left sided heart failure in older patients.

Hypoxia is the main concern in asthmatics, when a patient gets tired from trying to breathe out the high levels of CO_2. This can be seen as increase CO_2 levels on an ABG, this can result in death if not managed properly.

A low peak flow which when given a bronchodilator and the repeated peak flow increases by 12% is confirmation of asthma.

Relievers

Beta 2 adrenoceptor agonist:
Salbutamol (short acting) 2.5 -5 mg QDS   *Salmeterol* (long acting)
(side effect of palpitations) (lowers K$^+$)

Anti-muscarinic bronchodilators:
Ipratropium (short acting) 0.5mg OD   *Tiotropium* (long acting)

Preventers

Inhaled Corticosteroids or give oral *prednisolone*

Beclomethasone
Budesonide
Fluticasone
Beconase (nasal steroid spray)

Combination therapy

Seretide which is *Flixotide + Salmeterol*

Advise patients to lose weight, avoid pets and stop smoking. Also remember that obesity, NSAID's and aspirin aggravates asthma.

Asthma attacks

Remember **OBISMA**:

- **O**xygen
- **B**eta $_2$ agonist
- **I**V steroids
- **M**agnesium sulphate
- **A**minophylline

Initially patients can take 2-10 puffs within 10-20 minutes.

It is also important to monitor a patients ECG as both magnesium sulphate and aminophylline can cause ECG changes.

Chronic obstruction of the lung airflow which is not fully reversible and therefore may not respond to a bronchodilator. Most cases are smokers. [Aim for their O_2 saturation to be 88%-92%]

Symptoms	Signs
• Chronic cough with grey thick sputum • Shortness of breath (SOB) • Wheeze and quiet breath sounds • Reduced exercise tolerance • CO_2 retention flap • Central cyanosis • Pitting oedema	• Hypoxia • JVP raised from pulmonary hypertension • Hyperextended chest 'Barrel chest' • Laterally displaced heart (from hypertrophy)/(cor pulmonale) • Crackles and expiratory wheeze

A "pink puffer" is a person with emphysema that results from destruction of the airways distal to the terminal bronchiole and also includes the gradual destruction of the pulmonary capillary beds, thus decreased ability to oxygenate the blood.

A "blue bloater" has chronic bronchitis caused by excessive mucus production with airway obstruction resulting from hyperplasia of mucus-producing glands, goblet cell metaplasia, and chronic inflammation around bronchi.

Treatment

24%-28% via Venturi Mask

Salbutamol 5mg nebulised

Steroid e.g. *prednisolone* or IV *Hydrocortisone*

IV antibiotics

Short term

Short acting muscarinic agonist e.g. *Ipratropium bromide*

Long acting muscarinic agonist e.g. *Tiotropium*

Long term oxygen therapy

Stop smoking (20 per day = 1 pack year)

Long term

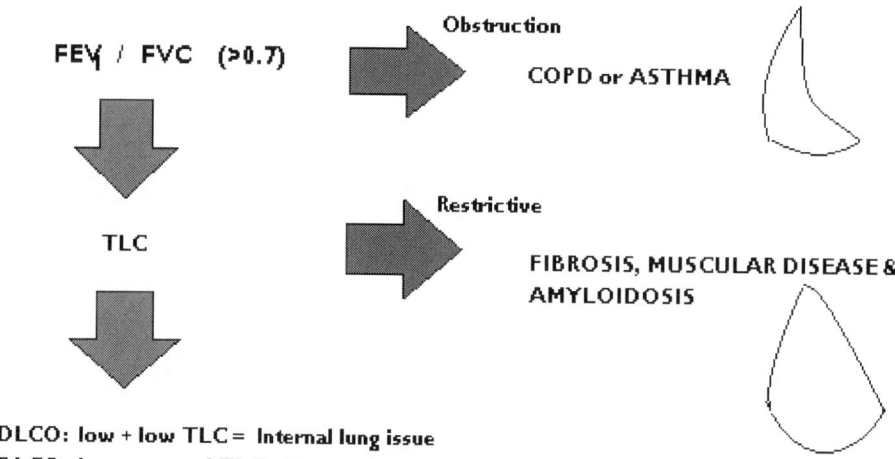

FEV / FVC (>0.7)

Obstruction

COPD or ASTHMA

TLC

Restrictive

FIBROSIS, MUSCULAR DISEASE & AMYLOIDOSIS

DLCO: low + low TLC = Internal lung issue
DLCO: low + normal TLC = Vascular issue (e.g Pulmonary hypertension)
DLCO: normal + low TLC = External lung issue (e.g Diaphragm/neuromuscular)
DLCO: normal + normal TLC = Non-pulmonary cause

- Causes an expiratory wheeze from airway oedema, try to intubate the patient unless they have trismus
- They can also present with a swollen tongue from angioedema
- Rashes can sometimes be seen particularly on the chest

Treat immediately with:

-Adrenaline (1:1000) (side effect is fluid overload- high blood pressure)

-Steroids (200mg IV)

-Antihistamine (*Chloramphenamine*)

-Fluids

EMPHYSEMA

On X-ray, there is a thin mediastinum, flat diaphragm and hyper inflated lungs (You can see more than 5 ribs anteriorly and more than 7 ribs posteriorly)

Check for any inherited alpha-1 antitrypsin deficiency.

TUBERCULOSIS

Symptoms:

- Cough lasting longer than 2 weeks with or without haemoptysis
- From a high risk area
- Fever at night
- Drenching night sweats
- Weight loss

X-Ray: Gohn focus (caseous necrosis, usually in lower or middle lobes) / Gohn complex (Gohn focus + lymphatic involvement). In secondary TB there would be a cavitating lesion (usually seen in upper lobes)

Disseminated /Miliary TB = abscesses in the kidneys and liver as well as a spotted chest X-Ray.

Treatment

Streptomycin, isoniazid, Ethambutol, rifampicin, pyrazidomide (multiple drugs to prevent Multiple drug resistant TB)

Side effects: Red/Orange urine (*rifampicin*), optic neuritis, peripheral neuropathy, skin rash, joint pain, nausea and vomiting.

Causes:

1. H.Pylori
2. NSAIDs (Side effect on Kidney, Stomach, Heart)
3. Smoking/Stress
4. Steroids
5. Alcohol

Stomach acid is made from proton pumps which involves H^+/K^+ ATPase pumps in parietal cells. The cells are stimulated by Acetylcholine, Histamine, and Gastrin.

H_2 antagonists act on enterochromafin cells stopping them releasing histamine. Low acid though causes the release of gastrin which then causes acid to be released anyway. Therefore proton pump inhibitors (PPI's) are used to kill off the entire pump.

Signs:

- Iron deficiency anaemia due to blood loss
- Abdominal pain

Treatment

Omeprazole (Proton pump inhibitor) (PPI side effect causes diarrhoea, nephritis and low magnesium)

Amoxicillin

Clarithromycin

Engorged veins in the oesophagus rupturing.

Requires immediate blood transfusion, *Ocraotide* (somatostatin), *vasopressin*, band ligation or balloon tamponade. Patients should also be given vitamin K and fresh frozen plasma to improve clotting.

It is important to always maintain the airways in these patients as they can aspirate from the bleeding. Failure to control active bleeding may require the introduction of an endotracheal tube.

Crohn's disease is an inflammatory bowel disease (IBD - Crohn's, ulcerative colitis and microscopic colitis) in which the body has an autoimmune attack. It has an association with smokers and commonly affects the terminal part of the ileum (where bile is absorbed) but can affect from the mouth to the anus. It occurs in patches called 'skip lesions' with transmural inflammation.

Symptoms:

- Abdominal pain/masses in iliac fossa
- Weight loss
- Nausea and vomiting
- Fistulas (from intestine to skin, bladder or vagina causing UTI's)

Signs:

- FBC – anaemia (ulcerated bowel results in the blood)
- B_{12} and Folate is often deficient

Treatment

5-aminoSalicylic acid e.g. *Mesalazine/Sulfasalazine/Osalazine* (side effects of diarrhoea)

Azathioprine/Mercaptoprine (also given Allopurinol to protect liver)

Prednisolone   {for mild to severe inflammation}

Budesonide   {for mild to severe inflammation}

Immunosuppressant's e.g. *Cyclosporine* (check magnesium and Cholesterol are not low or it can cause fits in combination with *Cyclosporine*)

If severe use *Methotrexate* and then consider surgery.

ULCERATIVE COLITIS

This condition is similar to Crohn's disease but occurs in continuous stretches of the colon starting from the rectum up. It is not transmural and instead only has mucosal and submucosal involvement, leaving the muscularis safe but causes pseudopolyps. Therefore, there is a cancer risk and screening is required.

It is also the most common cause of bloody diarrhoea. In a patient with an established diagnosis of ulcerative colitis, the features of an acute severe exacerbation are passing 6 or more bowel motions with blood in 24 hours plus any signs of haemodynamic instability, fever or inflammation (CRP/ESR).

Investigations

Bloods and stool culture (check for C.difficile toxin)

Endoscopy

Abdominal X-ray (toxic megacolon is indicated by a transverse colon diameter >6cm)

DIVERTICULITIS

Formed from low fibre diets which causes rough contractions that can lead to pushing of the inner intestinal lining out towards the muscle wall (Diverticulosis). These pockets can cause the segments of the bowel to have reduced movement as the muscle is now out pouched. Therefore causing diarrhoea, constipation or bloating.

If these pockets rupture or become infected it results in diverticulitis and diverticular bleeding.

Symptoms:

- Abdominal pain/ cramping
- Constipation
- Diarrhoea

Rupture of an infected diverticular can cause infection of the surrounding tissue causing diverticulitis which can lead to abscesses usually in the pelvic region.

Diverticular bleeding occurs when the expanding diverticulum erodes into a blood vessel. This can result in the passage of dark stool and clots or blood (melaena) without any abdominal pain.

When diverticulitis related infections spread outside of the colon, the colon tissues may stick to surrounding tissues causing adhesions. It can involve the bladder or small intestine, causing long lasting infections of the urinary tract. Fistulas may also form.

Treatment

Ciprofloxacin (penicillin allergy) and *metronidazole*

Or *Amoxicillin*

Laxatives to maintain flow and prevent any collection in pouches

Surgery required if the lumen narrows, recurrent infections, bleeds or fistulae. Adhesions may make surgery difficult and the patient is likely to need a stoma if no healthy bowel can be found to anastomose.

Alcoholic fatty liver disease (AFLD)	Non-alcoholic fatty liver disease (NAFLD)
Fatty liver (steatosis) ↓ Hepatitis (> Transaminases) ↓ Fibrosis (scar tissue) ↓ Cirrhosis (Necrotic tissue) shrinks(LFT's normalise towards the end stage)	Fatty liver (steatosis) ↓ Hepatitis ↓ Fibrosis (excess fat, not much function loss) ↓ Cirrhosis (nodular and fatty)
Symptoms -Severe jaundice (cannot process bilirubin) -Bleeding (reduced vitamin K for clotting) -Oedema (cannot produce enough albumin) -Ascites (can develop due to a loss of albumin) -Pruritus (from excess bilirubin) -Fibrosis causes obstruction to the portal blood flow which results in a back pressure in the venous return which can therefore cause oesophageal varices (these can rupture). -Caput medusa (check it's not an IVC blockage) - High HbA1c, high cholesterol, high GGT, low B_{12} therefore high MCV	Symptoms -Usually only very late stage NAFLD has signs -Right upper quadrant pain -Tiredness -Ultrasound gives a bright liver from fat reflection -Albumin decrease -Fibrosis causes obstruction to the portal blood flow which results in a back pressure in the venous return which can therefore cause oesophageal varices (these can rupture).
Treatment Reduce diet fats (interferes with alcohol metabolism) Supplement B_{12}, folate, calcium and iron. Beta blockers to reduce risk of portal hypertension. Lactulose to reduce ammonia absorption.	Treatment No drug treatment only standard lifestyle management e.g. exercise and dietary changes (NAFL can also be a side effect of methotrexate)

ALT + AST, PT, INR = high if liver cells are damaged

ALT higher than ALP= Hepatitis

Causes: viral (Hepatitis A/B, malaria, mononucleosis (glandular fever)), drug (paracetamol), ischaemia in hypotension, secondary tumours, sarcoidosis, primary biliary cirrhosis (autoimmune attack against the mitochondria), right heart failure e.g. cor pulmonale causing back pressure.

Signs: dark urine, normal stool

ALP higher than ALT= Gall bladder blocked (called cholestasis). You should also check GGT as bone and placenta also makes ALP

Causes: stones (painful), Pancreatic cancer (no pain because no stone. Instead the pancreatic head swells blocking the bile duct)

Signs: dark urine, pale stool (almost white! floats due to fat not being broken down because no bile is able to get into stool)

Investigation

Do ultrasound in both situations

Migratory pain (dull epigastric which becomes sharp constant right iliac fossa pain)

- Mild fever
- Anorexia
- Nausea
- Leucocytosis

Be sure to rule out ectopic pregnancies by checking the last monthly period and hCG.

If the patient is elderly then you should also consider cancer of the caecum.

Treatment

Nil by mouth, analgesia (and antiemetic), Fluids, FBC, LFT, U+E, Catheter. Finally surgery.

On X-ray you should not be able to view the small bowel. In an obstruction the usual haustrae present as plicae circulares. Also no air will be present in the large bowel indicating there is an obstruction.

Causes:

-Adhesions from previous surgery (Treatment = Gastrografin)

-Hernia

-Volvulus (Treatment = flatus tube)

-Band

-In wall (Ulcerative colitis, tumour, Diverticular stricture, Ischaemic stricture)

-In lumen (Bezoar, Intussusception, Gall stone in caecal valve)

Symptoms:

- Colicky abdominal pain
- Vomiting
- Distention (aerophage)
- Bowels have not opened and no flatus
- Fever if bowel has perforated
- Rebound tenderness indicates peritonitis
- Dehydration from the ileus shedding water into the 3rd space
- Rebound tachycardia

Investigation and treatment

Nasogastric tube to aspirate and prevent vomiting

Nil by mouth, analgesia (and antiemetic), fluids, bloods to assess dehydration, LFT, U+E, Catheter, CT to identify level of obstruction.

Treated with a stent or by-pass

Symptoms of ischemic colitis include severe abdominal pain and the passage of blood and mucus. An acute abdomen can develop with generalized abdominal pain, rigidity and ileus. Shock can also develop leading to acidosis and hypotension. X-Ray of ischemic colitis may show 'thumb-printing' and dilation of the small bowel. Treatment involves a surgical angioplasty to widen the blocked artery or to place a stent to bypass the blockage.

Acute pancreatitis: Abdominal pain radiating to the back, sometimes accompanied by a pruritus.

PO_2 <60, Age >55, Neutrophil >15, Calcium <2, Renal urea >16, Enzyme LDH >600, Amylase >85, Sugar >10. Checking faecal elastase and blood amylase are the most used test.

Treatment is fluids and analgesia.

Chronic pancreatitis can result in a critical amount of damage to both the endocrine and exocrine functions of the pancreas. Without the exocrine function of the pancreas, fat-soluble vitamins (A, D, E, K) cannot be digested. Malabsorption of fats will result in steatorrhea. Malabsorption will also result in:

A = night blindness

D = hypocalcemia

E = neurologic deficits and ataxia (very uncommon)

K = prolonged PT/aPTT

Direct (medial to inferior epigastric artery)	Indirect (lateral to inferior epigastric artery)
(in superficial ring)	(in superficial and deep ring)
Hernial sac parallel to spermatic cord	Hernial sac within spermatic cord

Symptoms: pain when standing, laying and walking

Treatment

Surgically push back and mesh over. Risks involve infection, haematoma (appears like a hernia), recurrence, colon damage, nerve damage, testis atrophy and death of testis.

Umbilical hernia: Similar symptoms and treatment with the additional risks of seroma (fluid pocket which may last a long time) and removal of belly button if the hernia is found to have adhesions anteriorly.

ANAL CANCER

Risk factors: Human papilloma virus 16/18, smoking and cervical cancer.

Symptoms: Pruritus, bleeding, pain, discharge and incontinence.

Investigation: MRI of the rectum / Proctoscopy / Rigid sigmoidoscopy

Treatment

Chemotherapy / surgery (stoma)

ANAL PAIN

Causes: Fissure, Abscess, Prolapse, haemorrhoids, Pilonidal cyst, Perianal haematoma and Pruritus.

Treatment

Surgery / Drain / Acetone fissure filler / GTN cream for haemorrhoids

Haemorrhoids = 3,7,11   Tear = 6, 12   Prostate/Cervix = 6

Prostate findings:

- Enlarged and smooth (Benign prostatic hyperplasia (BPH))
- Hard and irregular surface (Cancer)
- Reduced tone (perform squeeze test to assess neurological function)

BENIGN PROSTATIC HYPERPLASIA

Treatment

Finasteride (affects hair growth and prostate) or Flutamide (affects prostate)

Surgical treatment = Transurethral resection of prostate (TURP) / Transurethral incision of prostate (TUIP)

UTI

Check urine for nitrates, leukocytes, protein and/or blood

Treatment: Ciprofloxacin/ Gentamicin/ Vancomycin/ Nitrofurantoin / Trimethoprim

Causes:

- UTI
- Kidney / Ureter / Bladder stone
- Neurological (Parkinson's / lesion / cauda equina)
- Mediations (Anticholinergic / Antispasmodic / Anti-histamine / Anti-depressants)
- Alcohol (young patients)
- Constipation (Likely in elderly patients where hard stool pushes against urethra and bladder)
- Benign prostatic hyperplasia (BPH)
- Vaginal prolapse
- Pancreatic cancer

Treatment: Catheter flush if blocked (10ml saline) / Lithotripsy (break up stones) / Measure PSA (prostate specific antigen, high levels can suggest cancer).

Treatment for renal colic: NSAID's first (as it may pass), *Morphine*, hydration.

URINARY INCONTINENCE

The inability to retain urine. Symptoms:

- Worse when coughing, sneezing, exercising (pressure symptoms)

Check for any abdominal masses by palpation, vaginal prolapse or atrophy

Treatment

- Pelvic floor exercises
- Anti-muscarinic e.g. *Oxybutynin/solifenacin*
- Mirabegron (thickens lining of bladder)
- Serotonin-noradrenaline reuptake inhibitor e.g. *Duloxetine*
- Surgery for Mid urethral sling.

Psychological anxiety or depression can cause a rapid loss of erection

Organic (gradual decrease in erection)	Non-organic
>80yrs old Ischaemic Spinal and pelvic injuries Multiple sclerosis Diabetes	New medication SSRI's Beta blockers Smoking Alcohol

Treatment for both causes = *Sildenafil* (Viagra)
OR sexual counselling for psychological causes
Cannot be taken with nitrates or patients with severe heart conditions.

Swelling	Pain
• Sebaceous cyst (superficial) • Epididymal cyst (along the cord) • Varicocele (discomfort after long standing) (feels like a bag of worms texture) • Hydrocele (cannot feel testes, only fluid)(transilluminatable) • Tumours (hard, non-tender, fixed to testes) (check LDH, AFP, hCG)	• Epididymitis/ Orchitis (Red, hotter than opposite, swollen, pain in cord, eased when elevated) (Check for STI's/Mumps) • Referred pain (Kidney/Bladder stone) • Hernia (if upper border of lump not found)(perform cough test) • Torsion Testes (A+E!)(Rapid pain onset, raised up, broad abdomen pain) (go to surgery within 3 hours)

Causes:

- Pyelonephritis (infected kidney)
- Goodpasteurs syndrome
- Glomerulonephritis
- Bladder cancer

- Benign prostatic hyperplasia
- Could appear like blood (rifampicin, rhabdomyolysis)

Diagnose: Urine dips / Ultrasound / Flexible cystoscopy / Intravenous urogram / CT (kidney stone)

BLOOD IN STOOL

Upper Gi bleed = dark blood, low haemoglobin, high urea

Lower Gi bleed = fresh bright, mixed in (Haemorrhoids, fistula, cancer)

E.coli o157 causes haemorrhagic diarrhoea.

Faecal calprotectin (determines IBD or cancer over IBS)

BOWEL CANCER

Symptoms:

- Anaemia
- Weight loss
- Change in bowel habits
- Diarrhoea
- Tenesmus (urgency to go but cannot excrete)

Tests: Colonoscopy / CT / Blood test for Carcinoembryonic antigen (CEA)

Polyps of >1cm are high risk

NON-PROGRESSIVE GLOMERULAR NEPHROPATHIES

Glomerulonephritis (GN) is a renal disease characterised by Inflammation and damage to the glomeruli. This allows proteins and/or blood to exit with urine.

Non proliferative GN tends to have anatomical changes such as abnormal podocytes, a thicker glomerular basement membrane, and sclerosing of segments of the glomeruli.

Urine dip: WBC + protein + red cell cast (blood vessels leak out red blood cells and they merge to form rods)

Treatment

Prednisolone (steroid)

Treat oedema also

PROGRESSIVE GLOMERULAR NEPHROPATHIES

Goodpasture's syndrome= Anti-glomerular basement membrane antibodies. This is a rare condition where anti-bodies attack the basement membrane in lung and kidneys which can cause bleeding from them both. Can be caused by cocaine inhalation. This disease is associated with HLA-DR2.

Symptoms:

- Coughing up blood and blood in the urine
- Oedema
- Hypertension

Treatment

Corticosteroids

Majorly treated with plasmapheresis (removing antibodies from blood)

Immunosuppressant (*cyclophosphamide, prednisone*)

NEPHROTIC SYNDROME

Nephrotic syndrome = 'O' in the word, therefore prOtein is lost.

Symptoms

- Frothy urine
- Proteinurina

This is the loss of albumin (gaps in the podocytes allow protein to leak through) therefore the low albumin levels reduce the blood oncotic pressure causing fluid to move out into the surrounding tissues. Due to the low albumin levels the liver compensates by increasing the albumin production. The side effect of this is that it also increases the production of lipids.

<u>Secondary causes</u>

SLE

Hep B & C, HIV

Diabetes Mellitus

<u>Treatment</u>

Blood pressure medication to reduce blood pressure and the amount of protein released in urine.

ACEi/ARB	(*Ramipril*) / (*Losartan, valsartan*)
Diuretics	(*furosemide*) / (*spironolactone*)
Cholesterol reduction	(*fluvastatin*) (The side effect of statins is joint pain)
Blood thinners	(*heparin, delta heparin, warfarin*)

NEPHRITIC SYNDROME

Nephritic syndrome occurs due to podocytes developing large pores which allows blood and protein to escape into the urine.

Symptoms

- Haematuria
- Low urine volume
- Heart failure
- Hypertension (possible headaches)

<u>Secondary causes</u>

- Post-streptococcal upper respiratory tract infection
- Lupus (SLE)
- Vasculitis

<u>Treatment</u>

ACEi/ARB   (*Ramipril*) / (*Losartan, valsartan*)

Low K+ and low Na+ diet.

Corticosteroids and other anti-inflammatory drugs

AKI = A rapid reduction in kidney function resulting in the failure to maintain fluid balance, electrolytes and acid-base balance. Always consider dehydration as a cause.

Symptoms and signs:

- Low *u*rine output (oliguria/anuria)
- High *u*rea, *n*itrogen and *c*reatinine in the blood
- Metabolic acidosis
- Oedema (therefore raised JVP)
- *C*onfusion
- *N*ausea & vomiting
- Reduced *K*+ (Muscle weakness and cardiac instability)
- Pericarditis (urea irritates lining)

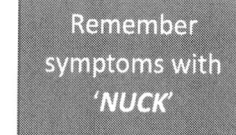

Remember symptoms with *'NUCK'*

Haemorrhage Cardiac failure NSAIDs, ACE Inhibitors, Hypertension Cirrhosis	**Pre Renal**
Glomerulitis Vasculitis Tubular necrosis (nephron necrosis due to ischaemia)	**Renal**
Bladder tumour Blood clots Kidney stones Blocked catheter	**Post Renal**

Treatment options:

- Fluid replacement
- Blood replacement (haemorrhage)
- Crystalloid (for Vomiting +Diarrhoea)

- Catheter + flush it + remove catheter
- Percutaneous nephrostomy

Investigations: Urine Na+, FBC, creatinine, ESR

Most patients will die of sepsis due to urea weakening the immune system.

CKD is the progressive loss of renal function over a period of months to years.

Symptoms (normally occur once GFR is below 30)

- Low urine output
- Vomiting
- Confusion
- Metallic taste
- Fatigue and anaemia (low erythropoietin)
- Shortness of breath (pulmonary oedema)
- >Respiratory rate
- >Heart rate
- >Blood pressure (fluid overload and release of vasoactive hormones)

Treatment

CKD stages 1&2 risk of cardiovascular death is higher than renal

| -ACEi/ARB | (*Ramipril*) / (*Losartan, valsartan*) |

-ACEi/ARB   (*Ramipril*) / (*Losartan, valsartan*)

-Statins   (*Fluvostatin*)

-Loop diuretics for oedema management   (*Furosemide*)

-Consider erythropoietin injections for anaemia

-Gabapentin to treat any restless legs

-Lastly Dialysis

CLOSTRIDIUM DIFFICILE

Profuse watery diarrhoea (which represents a change in bowel habit) + recent antimicrobial therapy.

- For non-severe cases clearly induced by antibiotic use, with no signs of severe colitis, it may be acceptable to stop antibiotic treatment and observe for 48 hours.
- Antibiotic treatment includes *metronidazole, vancomycin,* and *fidaxomicin.*

- For mild/moderate disease, oral *metronidazole*
- For severe patients, *vancomycin* or *fidaxomicin*
- Faecal transplantation is recommended for multiple recurrent C.diff infections

For patients with perforation and/or systemic inflammation despite antibiotic treatment, total abdominal colectomy or diverting loop ileostomy combined with colonic lavage is recommended.

Additional management measures include discontinuing unnecessary antimicrobial therapy, adequate replacement of fluids and electrolytes, avoiding anti-motility medications, and reviewing the use of proton pump inhibitors.

MRSA

The gold standard treatment is *vancomycin*

ANTIMICROBIALS

•Gram negatives:	•Gram positives:
−Amoxicillin	−Amoxicillin
−Gentamicin	−Gentamicin
−Co-amoxyclav	−Co-amoxyclav
−Cefuroxime	−Piperacillin/tazobactam
−Ciprofloxacin (Good for Pseudomonas)	−Vancomycin
−Piperacillin/tazobactam	
Anaerobes: −Metronidazole, Co-amoxyclav, Piperacillin/tazobactam	

•Gram negatives cocci:	•Gram positive cocci:
−N. gonorrhoea	−Staphylococci
	−Streptococci
•Gram negatives bacilli:	•Gram positive bacilli:
−E.coli	−Anthrax (aerobe)
−Salmonella	−Clostridium difficile (anaerobe)
−Haemophulius	

Diuretics	Common: postural hypotension, gout, urinary urgency; Serious: electrolyte imbalance (hypokalaemia, hypomagnesia, hyponatraemia), arrhythmia.
ACE inhibitors	Common: cough, hypotension including postural; Serious: worsening renal function, renal infarction in renal artery stenosis, angio-oedema
Beta-blockers	Common: tiredness, bradycardia, coldness. Serious: asthmatic attack, exacerbation of heart failure, heart block
Spironolactone	Common: gynaecomastia, tiredness, rashes; Serious: hyperkalaemia, hyponatraemia.
Digoxin	Common: nausea; Serious: life threatening arrhythmias
Angiotensin II receptor antagonists	Common: hypotension including postural; Serious: worsening renal function, renal infarction in renal artery stenosis
Amiodarone	Common: photosensitivity, nausea, thyroid dysfunction, sleep disturbance, corneal microdeposits; Serious: thyrotoxic storm, pro-arrhythmia, pulmonary/hepatic fibrosis.
Steroids	Nightmares, hunger, stomach irritation.

Obstetrics and Gynaecology

Normal timings:

12 Weeks- The bump is just palpable

16 Weeks- The fundus is half way between the umbilicus and pubic symphysis

20 Weeks- The fundus is nearing the umbilicus

22 Weeks- At the umbilicus

36 Weeks- At the xiphisternum

LMP = last monthly period

Expected due date (EDD) = first day of last Period + 9 months + 7 days

DIETARY SUPPLEMENTS

Folic acid is offered from pre-pregnancy to 12 weeks

Vitamin D is offered in pregnancies of non-white skin types

Ferrous sulphate is offered in twins or anaemia

GESTATIONAL DIABETES

These patients are at risk of worsening nephrology, neuropathy, pre-eclampsia and a caesarean section. It also causes there to be a larger placenta during pregnancy. Further risks include:

- Macrosomia
- Shoulder dystocia
- Polyhydramnios
- Still birth
- Neonatal hypoglycaemia
- Neonatal jaundice
- Neonatal respiratory distress

Stop oral hypoglycaemics (except metformin) and aim for a normal HbA1C. Give high dose *Folic Acid*, low dose *Aspirin*. If on insulin deliver baby at 38 Weeks.

Gestational diabetes is defined as a Fasting Glucose of >5.6mmol and Glucose Tolerance of >7.8mmol

FITS DURING PREGNANCY

Treat with *Magnesium Sulphate* (during labour and 24hrs after if pre-eclampsic)

Do not use *Valproate/Carbamazepine* as these can cause neural tube defects, foetal heart defects and develop delays in the growing foetus.

Do not use *Clobazam* as this can cause neonatal withdrawal

HYPERTENSION

Maternal hypertension = 140/90 on two occasions at least six hours apart. Severe hypertension = 160/110 mmHg

Treatment

Anti-hypertensives = *Labetalol* (Beta Blocker), *Methyl-dopa* (Alpha agonist), *Nifedipine* (Calcium antagonist). Check blood pressure and urine protein.

Aspirin should be given from 12 weeks until delivery. The best cure is to deliver the baby in case there is pathology with the placenta. Steroids are given for lung maturation if at or before 34 weeks.

Pre-eclampsia = Hypertension + Proteinuria (>20mg)

Eclampsia = Hypertension + proteinuria (>20mg) + seizures

Symptoms:

- Oedema
- Sharp liver pain or epigastric pain – can be a liver haematoma
- Low urine
- Increased reflexes (cerebral irritation)
- High uric acid (>380)
- Headache
- Disseminating intravascular coagulation (DIC)

Foetal effects:

- Small baby
- Foetal distress

Investigations: FBC (to see if platelets are affected), LFT, U+E, Uric Acid (oxidative stress) and Coagulation. [Collectively signs of end organ damage]

Treatment: Inducing labour if at 34 weeks gestation (dexamethasone for lung maturation if before 34 weeks).

ANAEMIA

Haemodilution takes place in pregnancy at 28 weeks, defined as Hb <110 in 2nd trimester and Hb <105 in 3rd trimester and postpartum. Usually anaemia causes:

- Inter Uterine Growth Restriction (IUGR)
- Preterm labour
- Postpartum haemorrhage (PPH)

Investigations: Family history, check for any bleeding sites and iron studies

Treatment

Iron 200mg TDS (IV if not tolerated), Folate, B12 and high protein diet. Blood transfusion if still persistent.

Platelets can be low due to pregnancy or due to a long standing immune related conditions. Platelets <130 but >100.

Usually takes place in the 3rd trimester but doesn't affect the baby.

Other causes:

- HELLP (haemolysis, elevated liver enzyme, low platelets)
- HIV
- Disseminating intravascular coagulation (DIC)
- Lupus (SLE)
- Leukaemia/Aplastic anaemia

Treatment

Steroid / IV Ig (<50) / splenectomy (Immune modulated)

Instrumental births should be avoided.

There are 3 types, 1, 2 and 3. Generally an autosomal dominant condition.

Symptoms and signs include increased bleeding time and low vWF levels (fortunately it increases during pregnancy).

Treatment

Desmopressin / Tranexamic acid / vWF concentrate

This is a haemolytic anaemia which is common in African, Caribbean and Middle Eastern people.

Main priority is not to allow for the patient to become dehydrated or hypoxic (sickle crisis), this should be treated with antibiotics, blood, O_2 and fluids.

Ensure adequate labour analgesia and serial growth scans of the foetus.

Treatment

Supplement *folate* (5mg/day). Vaccination (Pneumococcal + Meningococcal)

If there are frequent crisis treat them with *hydroxycarbamide*

DVT TO PE

Risk factors: High BMI, immobility, thrombophilia, family history, surgery, pregnancy. Postpartum is the highest risk for DVT/PE.

Treatment: Thromboembolism stockings and *Low molecular weight heparin* for 6 weeks postpartum.

UTI

It is very common for women to get urinary tract infections due to the suppression of the immune system during pregnancy.

Treatment:

1st Trimester

- *Cefradine* 500mg (QDS)
- *Trimethoprim* 200mg (not for use in 1st trimester due to folate deficiency) therefore + folic acid 5mg

1st + 2nd Trimester

- *Nitrofurantoin* 50mg (not for use in 3rd trimester due to haemolysis)
- *Sulphonamides* (not for 3rd trimester due to haemolysis methaemaglobinaemia)

2nd + 3rd Trimester

- *Trimethoprim* 200mg (not for use in 1st trimester due to folate deficiency)

If unable to treat the infection with the suggested antibiotics you should use *Amoxicillin* 250mg TDS

Premature separation of a normally situated placenta. Blood can collect behind the placenta or escape and present as per vagina (PV) bleeding.

Symptoms:

- Pain +/- PV bleeding
- Uterine contractions
- Enlarged 'woody hard' uterus (blood makes the uterus a hard sac)
- Difficulty identifying foetal parts (blood makes the uterus like a hard sac)
- Foetal heart abnormalities (distress)

Treatment

Caesarean section

Placenta partially or wholly situated within the lower uterine segment, crossing over the cervix. If seen before 32weeks then it is not strictly speaking a placenta praevia as there is no lower uterine segment before 32weeks (the placenta may raise later during the pregnancy as the uterus continues to grow in size).

Symptoms:

- Painless vaginal bleeding (can be provoked by intercourse)
- Hypotensive
- Non-tender uterus
- Normal foetal heart rate

Complications: Placenta acreta (placental growth into myometrium)/increta (growth into uterine wall)/percreta (growth through to bladder).

Treatment

Induction of labour / caesarean section

>500ml blood loss

Primary = <24 hours   Secondary = >24 hours   Massive = >2.5L

Tone- Uterine atony is the commonest cause. Under normal physiology uterine contractions after birth close down on the spiral blood vessels and stop the bleeding.

Tear- At any point between the uterus and the vulva

Tissue- Retained placental tissue or membranes, if left inside for too long the uterus will not be able to contract down.

Thrombin- DIC from the large loss of blood which causes a depletion of clotting factors.

Treatment:

Tone	Rub the uterus / Bimanual procedure E.g. *Oxytocin / Misoprostol / Carboprost / Ergometrine* (not if preeclampsic) Surgical: Bakri balloon / B-lynch sutures / Uterine artery embolization / hysterectomy
Tear	Suture
Tissue	Remove under general anaesthetic
Thrombin	Aggressively treat with blood transfusions

INDUCING LABOUR

- Membrane sweep (releases prostaglandins and irritates uterus to contract)
- Catheter induction (Foley catheter inserted through cervix, inflated with 30ml and leave in situ under traction for 12 hours)
- Prostaglandins e.g. *Dinoprostone*
- Artificial rupture of membranes

CARDIOTOCOGRAPH (CTG)

Remember 'C.BRAVAD': Contractions (how many in 10 minutes), Babies heart rate, Variability (Height of one peak to the next), Accelerations (rise in baseline by 15 for 15seconds), and Decelerations (drop in baseline by 15 for 15seconds)

CORD PROLAPSE

This is when a loop of umbilical cord slips below the foetal head. Often when amniotic fluid is low. Blood flow to the foetus is then compromised due to the compression of the cord. The lack of oxygen causes distress to the baby and causes CTG decelerations.

Treatment: Place gloved fingers into the vagina to push the foetus off the cord until C-section is possible. The mother can also do a knees to chest position combined with the Trendelenburg (head down) manoeuvre to move the baby.

Alternatively, use a catheter to fill the bladder to push the baby off the cord.

FOETAL BRADYCARDIA

A sudden drop in foetal heart rate for more than 3 minutes. The majority recover spontaneously.

3,6,9 RULE: call assistance at 3 minutes, prepare for delivery at 6 minutes, deliver baby by 9 minutes.

SHOULDER DYSTOCIA

Baby's anterior shoulder becomes obstructed against the mum's pubic bone.

Management: HELPER

- get Help
- Evaluate for episiotomy
- Lithotomy (legs to midline + towards ceiling + Laterally outward)
- Pressure on external abdomen
- Enter to perform internal manoeuvres (pull out opposite shoulder and arm)
- Rotate mother on to all fours

Can be mistaken for dermatological conditions such as Lichen Planus

- Vulva itching, soreness and irritation.
- Redness of the vagina and vulva.
- Vaginal discharge, often white (like cottage cheese) and this can be thick or thin but is usually odourless.
- Pain or discomfort during sex or when passing urine

You need two confirmed high vaginal swabs (lateral walls) out of 4 symptomatic episodes to be classified as recurrent.

Causes: Hyper/hypothyroidism, over washing the vagina or tight clothing

Investigations: Gram stains would show hyphae and spores

Treatment

Imidazole / nystatin / Clotrimazole cream (oral tablet form is teratogenic)

Or Canesten cream (*Clotrimazole*)

BACTERIAL VAGINOSIS

Due to an imbalance of the vaginal pH

- Homogenous white discharge stuck to walls of vagina
- Fishy odour
- Creates biofilm for bacteria
- Clue cells (full of bacteria)
- Risk for miscarriage and HIV

Investigations: KOH test for pH >5

Treatment (Partners need treating too)

Only if symptomatic/ pregnant/ poor obstetric history with *Metronidazole/Clindamycin* (allergy).

- Frothy
- Yellow discharge
- Dot haemorrhages (strawberry surfaces appearance)
- Can be itchy/sore or asymptomatic
- Can be passed mother to daughter but normally clears on own <1year

Investigation: Wet Prep swab (Posterior fornix), PCR

Treatment (Partners need treating too)

Metronidazole 2g (over 4-5 days if pregnant woman) (No alcohol 2 hours prior)

Damages the cilia in the fallopian tubes therefore creates a risk of ectopic pregnancy. Can be asymptomatic or present with:

- Pain
- Lower abdomen pain (check if the patient has IBD instead)
- Dysuria
- Bleeding
- Tender
- Cervical motion tenderness

Treatment

Antibiotics (*Erythromycin* 1g (7 days) + *Doxycycline* 100mg (10 days))

Or spontaneous clearing after 6 months but can lead to pelvic inflammatory disease (PID), conjunctivitis or reactive arthritis later in life.

Seen more in men than women. Women can have no symptoms and it can lead to pelvic inflammatory disease (PID) and reactive arthritis.

Symptoms:

- Sore throat
- Dyspareunia
- Dysuria
- Abdominal pain.

Need to perform NAAT 3 site checks (Anus, Genitalia, and Mouth). In order to perform this test the patient should not have passed urine 1-2 hours prior.

Treatment

Ceftriaxone 500 (IM) / *Spectinomycin* (IM) (if allergic to *Cephalosporins*) + *Azithromycin*

PELVIC INFLAMMATORY DISEASE

Must first exclude UTI, ectopic, ruptured cyst, gonorrhoea and chlamydia.

- Dull pain or tenderness in the stomach or lower abdominal area, or pain in the right upper abdomen.
- Abnormal vaginal discharge that is yellow or green in colour or has an unusual odour
- Painful urination
- Chills or high fever
- Nausea and vomiting
- Dyspareunia
- Cervical motion tenderness

Treatment

Doxycycline (teratogenic)/ *Azithromycin* + *Ceftriaxone* + *Metronidazole*

Find out if the patient wishes to have periods at all. Try to treat the main cause.

Symptomatic pain relief:

- *Mefenamic acid* 500mg TDS
- *Tranexamic acid* 1g TDS

Types include: Intramural, pedunculated, submucosal and subserosal – these two can press into the perineal space.

Symptoms: menorrhagia, pain, pressure pain (from coughing, standing or sneezing)

Treatment

Shrinking: *Goserelin* 3.6mg (GnRH agonist) (Short term effect)

   Ulipristil 5mg TDS (Selective progesterone receptor modulator) (permanent effect)

Surgery: Myomectomy/uterine artery embolization

Endometrial tissue growing outside of the uterus. Usually over the ovaries, adnexa and behind the uterus along the pouch of Douglas.

Symptoms:

- Cyclical pain
- Pelvic pain
- Dyschezia
- Dyspareunia
- Infertility
- Bimanual tenderness
- Fixed uterus
- Nodular uterus

Diagnosed laparoscopically

Treatment

Initially- COCP/ POP/ GnRH agonist/ LHRH. Surgical- Excision/ablation.

POLYCYCSTIC OVARIES SYNDROME

The result of an ovary which is unable to push out an egg each month to travel down the fallopian tubes. This results in many follicles (eggs) stuck inside the ovary. The egg however does mature and releases oestrogen. These levels rise pass threshold to cause a positive feedback effect on the anterior pituitary's release of LH and negative effect on FSH. This causes a high LH: FSH ratio. The maturing stroma over the eggs releases androgens which gives:

- Hertism
- Hair growth along inner lines of chest and legs
- Acne
- Irregular menstruation
- Infertility (egg never released)
- High testosterone
- High LH:FSH ratio
- High insulin (causes the ovaries to produce more testosterone)
- Low sex hormone binding globulin (therefore more free testosterone)

Treatment

Symptoms	1st line	2nd line
Menstrual abnormalities and hirsutism/acne	• Oral contraceptive pill	• Spironolactone (Androgen antagonist)
Infertility	• Clomiphene	• Letrozole or bilateral ovarian drilling of stroma
Metabolic/glycaemic abnormalities and for improving menstrual irregularities	• Metformin (teratogenic)	

TUMOUR TESTS

Ca125 test (ovarian cancer), Ca153 (Breast cancer), hCG, LDH, AFP and Inhibin are also useful tests in testicular tumours

Caused by the rupture, bleed or torsion (twist) of an ovary. Torsion can cut off blood supply and cause necrosis.

Symptoms include acute pelvic pain. Diagnosed with ultrasound.

Analgesia must be given if in pain but treatment is ultimately laparoscopic surgery.

CONTRACEPTION

Method and side effects	Action	Contraindication
Combined Oestrogen + Progesterone (COCP) Weight gain, mood changes, tender breast	Ovulation Cervical mucus Endometrial growth	VTE, CVD, Ca Cervix, Ca Breast, migraines with aura. -VTE 1st degree relative -Anti-TB/CF drugs -Anti-convulsive drugs
Progesterone only pill (POP) Cerelle/Cerezett or minipills Erratic bleeding	Ovulation Cervical mucus (minipills)	Breast cancer, Liver disease Needs to be taken within 12 hour / 3 hour window (mini pill)
Progesterone only implant (LARC) Erratic bleeding, itching at implant	Ovulation	
Progesterone only injections Depo provera (IM)/(SC) Weight gain, delays fertility for 1 year	Ovulation	VTE, CVD, Liver disease, <Bone density (teenagers/elderly)
Intrauterine coils (IUS) Copper coil Hormonal coil	Toxic foreign body	Breast Cancer (hormonal coil) Does not prevent ectopic
Emergency Contraceptive Levonelle EllaOne Copper IUD	Ovulation Hormone modulator Toxic 5-19 days post	

Pharmaceutical:

Less than 9 weeks   *Mifepristone* (Progesterone antagonist)

2 days later   *Misoprostol* (Induces uterine contractions)

Surgical:

Less than 12 weeks   Manual vacuum

More than 22 weeks   Feticide (k+ injection to heart)

It is normal to bleed up to 4 weeks after an abortion. If bleeding persists or positive hCG levels then consider:

- Failed abortion
- Retained products of conception
- Sepsis/Chlamydia
- New pregnancy/Ectopic

Types of miscarriage

Threatened

-Vaginal bleeding

-Closed Os

-Foetal cardiac activity

Missed

-No vaginal bleeding

-Closed Os

-Empty sac/ no heart rate

Inevitable

-Vaginal bleeding

-Dilated Os

-Products of conception seen

Incomplete

-Vaginal bleeding

-Dilated Os

-Some retained products

 of conception

Complete

-Vaginal bleeding/ none

-Closed Os

-Expelled all products

 of conception

Breast tissue becomes inflamed and painful, usually within the first 3 weeks after birth. 2 types of mastitis exist:

- Lactation mastitis/puerperal mastitis (caused by infection)
- Periductal mastitis (non-breast feeding women)

Symptoms:

- Usually unilateral
- Red, swollen, may feel hot, painful
- Breast lumps or areas of hardness
- Pain while feeding child
- Discharge may be white/blood
- Flu like symptoms

Treatment

Allow baby to suckle and it will clear the duct. Milk remains sterile.

NIPPLE THRUSH

Symptoms:

- Cracked, flaky, tender
- Areola is red an shiny
- Shooting pains in towards inner breast centre
- Itching
- Pain while breast feeding
- Child will have oral thrush

Treatment

Clotrimazole cream 1%, discard milk.

BREAST CANCER

Most will be surgically removed if invasive but treatment up to that point aims to prevent the growth of the tumour by inhibiting their response to oestrogen. This is done by blocking their receptors however other organs of the body with oestrogen receptors can be activated by the same drug while the breasts are inactivated (E.g. *Tamoxifen* caused proliferation of the endometrium risking endometrial cancer whilst reducing breast cancer). The currently used drug is now *Raloxifen* which doesn't stimulate the endometrium.

Ask: Arterial supply of breast = Axillary, Subclavian, Intercostal

-how many pregnancies

-menopause

-type of periods

-menarche

-breastfeeding

Genetic testing can be conducted to try to identify strong causative factors such as the BRCA-1 gene. With mutations of both BRCA-1 and BRCA-2 genes women are at high risk of breast and ovarian cancer. The best treatment is prophylactic bilateral mastectomy in these patients because of the BRCA-1 inheritance. Bilateral oophorectomy should also be considered.

POSTPARTUM BLUES

Usually takes place around day 3-5 postpartum and this is associated with the rapid decline of hormones involved with pregnancy that can cause a sudden decrease in mood and energy. It can also take place any time during the first year.

GP and
Mental Health

Main causes:

-Parkinson's diseases (degeneration of midbrains substantia nigra which is the source of dopamine)

-Drugs (anti-dopaminergics, schizophrenic drugs, valproate)

-Toxin (manganese, MTPT)

-Cerebrovascular disease

-Atoxic brain injury

-Traumatic brain injury

-Post-encephalitis

Symptoms:

- Asymmetrical resting tremor
- Rigidity(spasticity)
- Gait – short steps, shuffling, no arm swings, hands frozen
- Posture – bent forward
- Turning on the spot takes more than 3 steps
- Autonomic symptoms – impotence, postural dizziness, urinary incontinence, loses sense of smell (1st sense to go)
- Slurred speech/quieter/monotone
- Dysphagia
- Poker face
- Dementia
- Reduced blinking, bradykinesia

Treatment: *Levodopa, monoamine oxidase inhibitor* (MOA-B), *Catechol-o-methyltransferase inhibitor* (COMT), *Dopamine receptor agonist*

This is the most common type of tremor and can sometimes be mistaken for the parkinsonian resting tremor. It is autosomal dominant and not curable.

Symptoms:

-Action tremor

-Postural tremor

-Affects head, voice, Jaw

-Improved with Alcohol

-Better at rest

Treatment

Beta Blockers / *Primidone* (anti-convulsion)

Types:

- Alzheimer's (most common) - short term memory loss and personality change
- Vascular (from hypertension/COPD/diabetes/stroke) step down progression of baseline
- Mixed
- Frontotemporal - language + speech + writing /behaviour affected
- Lewy body and Parkinson - hallucinations are common

These changes can be seen on brain MRI's. Most patients will die of aspiration pneumonia due to loss of swallow function.

Lewy Body Dementia

Parkinson + Severe dementia

Multiple System Atrophy

Parkinson + Autonomic features + postural BP

Corticobasal Degeneration

Parkinson + Dysphagia

All 'Parkinson-Plus' (red) conditions:

- Respond poorly to Levodopa
- more progressive – early falls
- symmetrical, early symptoms

Parkinson + dementia + backward neck tilt + limited eye movements (supranuclear gaze palsy where they cannot look up) + usually fall backwards.

Extra pyramidal symptoms can be present such as dystonia (continuous spasms and muscle contractions), akathisia (motor restlessness), parkinsonism (characteristic symptoms such as rigidity), bradykinesia (slowness of movement), and tardive dyskinesia (irregular, jerky movements).

ACUTE STRESS REACTION

An immediate stress response to an event and usually diminishes in 48 hours.

Management: Protection (tell them the threat is gone), reassurance, screen for other problems, watch and wait (1 month GP review in case PTSD)

ADJUSTMENT DISORDER

After a big life changing event or soon after (less than 1 month after).

Symptoms:
- Autonomic arousal
- Anxiety
- Dramatic
- Self-harm
- Substance misuse
- Misbehaving (children)

It is a diagnosis of exclusion so you must rule out anxiety or depression first.

Management: Counselling referral / Anxiolytics (for short term use)

Treatment

Removal of stressor (usually resolves in a similar time frame to the change)

Depressed mood + loss of enjoyment (anhedonia) + reduced energy (anergia). Patients usually have a lack of motivation to get up and everything becomes a huge effort for them.

Also check if it is a delusion of self-impression by testing their belief

<u>Treatment</u>

Cognitive behavioural therapy (CBT) if the patient has mild depression

Drugs to be used only if depression is severe:

Citalopram/ Sertraline /Fluoxetine /Escitalopram (SSRI's) (side effects include dry eyes, dry mouth, low Na$^+$)

Mirtazapine (atypical)

Lithium (augmentation)

Rare condition

A delusional, worsened state of depression. All symptoms worsen to the point of no activity (stupor) or over activity, avoiding food/water and hallucinations.

Chronic disorder, sometimes described as 'manic depression'.

It is important to ask 'have you felt high at points?' as this condition presents with depression and episodes of feeling belated.

Anti-depressants should **not** be used because it can cause manic episodes

Management involves mood stabilising drugs e.g. *Lithium / Carbamazepine*

A belated mood with decreased need for sleep and high flow of thoughts. E.g. applying for many jobs or spending sprees.

Causes:

- Illicit drugs
- Steroids
- Hyperthyroidism

SCHIZOPHRENIA

- Delusions (positive sign)
- Hallucinations (positive sign)
- Disorganized speech (positive sign)
- Disorganized or catatonic behaviour (negative sign)
- Social isolation/poor self-care (negative sign)

You are more likely to develop schizophrenia if there is a family history of the illness. The twin of a person with schizophrenia has a 50% chance of developing schizophrenia.

Anti-psychotic treatment
- *Haloperidol*
- *Chlorpromazine* (works on M,HT,H receptor blockers)
- *Flupenthixol decanoate* (depot injection)

Atypical treatment (more selective in their dopamine blockade and also block serotonin 5 HT2 receptors)

- *Clozapine*
- *Olanzapine*

Always ensure the patient is seen by the mental health team prior to the prescribing of any medication for their longterm management.

This disorder is characterized by excessive anxiety and worry about a number of events and activities. Worrying is difficult to control. Anxiety and worry are associated with at least 3 of the following 6 symptoms occurring more days than not for at least 6 months:

- Restlessness or feeling keyed-up or on edge
- Being easily fatigued
- Difficulty concentrating or mind going blank
- Irritability
- Muscle tension
- Sleep disturbance

Treatment

CBT generally includes self-reward as well as problem solving and can be as effective as medications, especially for children with mild generalized anxiety disorder.

Selective serotonin reuptake inhibitors (SSRIs) are generally used as first-line agents, followed sometimes by tricyclic antidepressants (TCAs).

-Short term symptom relief can be treated *propranolol*

-*Citalopram*(celexa)   -*Escitalopram*(lexapro)   -*Paroxetine*(paxil)   -*Fluoxetine* (prozac)

-*Amitriptyline*

A panic attack is an abrupt period of intense fear accompanied by 4 or more of the following 13 systemic symptoms:

- Palpitations, pounding heart, or accelerated heart rate
- Sweating
- Trembling or shaking
- Shortness of breath or feeling of smothering
- Feelings of choking
- Chest pain
- Nausea or abdominal distress
- Feeling dizzy or faint
- Chills or heat sensations
- Paraesthesia

Reassure and calm the patient. Untreated panic attacks can subside spontaneously within 20-30 minutes, especially with reassurance and a calming environment.

DELIRIUM

Acute loss of attention and/or loss of consciousness. Variable mood which can be withdrawn or misbehaving or sleepy.

2 types:

Hypoalert (common)	Hyperalert (rare)
Underactive	Overactive
Sleepy	Belligerent
Not eating	Aggressive

Causes: Systemically unwell, medication, Wernicke's, poisoning, electrolyte imbalance, arrhythmia, hypoxia, constipation and pain.

PERSONALITY DISORDER

Abnormalities may be in the frontal, temporal, and parietal lobes. It may be caused by perinatal injury, encephalitis, trauma or genetics. It is also associated with monoamine oxidase and serotonin neurotransmitters.

- Expected abandonment
- Unstable and intense interpersonal relationships
- Unstable self-image
- Impulsivity that are potentially self-damaging - e.g., sex or substance abuse
- Recurrent suicidal behaviours or threats or self-mutilation
- Feelings of emptiness
- Inappropriate and intense anger
- Paranoia or dissociation

Treatment

Dialectic behaviour therapy (DBT), a modification of standard cognitive-behavioural techniques.

Selective serotonin reuptake inhibitors (SSRIs) are greatly preferred to the other classes of antidepressants; they can reduce impulsivity and aggression.

- Orderliness, perfectionism, and control which interferes with efficiency, despite the individual's focus on tasks
- Lack of flexibility
- Reluctance to delegate tasks
- An excessive devotion to work, with the exclusion of leisure activity
- Often, inflexibility with regard to matters of morality, ethics, and values to a point beyond cultural norms
- In many cases, stinginess and stubbornness

Treatment: CBT / SSRI's antidepressants (*fluoxetine / sertraline / citalopram*)

AUTISM

Autism spectrum disorder (ASD) is characterized by abnormalities in social interactions, communication skills, and restricted repetitive behaviours, interests, and activities.

- Developmental delays
- Poor reactions to environmental stimuli
- Poor social interactions
- Lack of smiling when greeted by parents and other familiar people
- Atypical responses to pain and physical injury
- **Language and writing delays**
- Susceptibility to infections and febrile illnesses
- **Repetitive behaviour**

Medications used in managing related behavioural problems and comorbid conditions in children with autism include the following:

- Second-generation antipsychotics (e.g. *risperidone / ziprasidone / aripiprazole,*)
- SSRI antidepressants (e.g. *fluoxetine / citalopram / escitalopram*)
- Stimulants (e.g. *methylphenidate*)

Attention deficit hyperactivity disorder (ADHD) is a developmental condition of inattention and distractibility, with or without accompanying hyperactivity.

Inattentive =

- Fails to give close attention to details or makes careless mistakes in schoolwork, work, or other activities
- Difficulty sustaining attention in tasks or play activities
- Does not seem to listen to what is being said
- Cannot follow through on instructions and fails to finish schoolwork, chores, or duties in the workplace (not because of a failure to understand the instructions given to them)
- difficulties organizing tasks and activities

Hyperactivity =

- Fidgeting
- Leaving seat in situations which remaining seated is expected
- Running about or climbing excessively
- Difficulty playing or engaging in activities quietly
- Excessive talking

Treatment

Stimulants are the first-line therapy and the most effective treatment (*Methylphenidate/ Dextroamphetamine*)

SUICIDE

Check: - friends(protective)   -religion(protective)   -family   -thought about it   -planned it?

Risk factor:

1. History of Self harm
2. Worthless
3. Nothing to look forward to
4. Family history
5. Depression/Anxiety
6. Male
7. Alcohol/drug
8. Having children (protective)

Vascular/electric events = sudden

Migraine = slowly spreads (can cause visual and sensory loss)

Infection/Inflammation events = Hours/Days

Degenerative/cancerous events = Weeks

Upper neuron weakness:

- Babinski
- Rigidity
- Hyperreflexia (Brisk)
- Hypertonia
- Weakness

Lower neuron weakness:

- Hypotonic
- Weakness
- Wasting
- Fasciculation
- Hyperreflexia

GUILLIAN BARRÉ

Usually an acute neurological deficit (less than 4 weeks)

Immune mediated attack of the peripheral nervous system. Often follows viral infection (Epstein Barr virus or Campylobacter). Inflammation causes weakness in all the limbs, usually distal to proximal, as well as dysphagia and facial weakness.

Symptoms: Pain, paraesthesia, dysautonomia (cardiac, BP, and bladder affected)

Monitor functional vital capacity (< 1L is very poor). If the patient also suffers facial weakness then use a face mask to assist with breathing.

Treatment

IV Ig / Plasma exchange (50% faster recovery)

Mixed, upper and lower neurons degenerate (e.g. wasting of muscle but with heightened reflexes)

Example symptoms

- Slurred speech
- Saliva pooling
- Tongue wasting and fasciculation's
- Brisk jaw jerk
- Hand wasting
- Can have dropped head (weakness)

Investigation: Check creatinine kinase (muscle / nerve damage)

Treatment

Anti-spasmodic (*hyoscine* patch) / *Atropine* / CPAP / *Rilazole* (inhibits glutamate) / Enteral feeding.

MYASTHENIA GRAVIS

Essential muscle fatigue. An autoimmune condition against calcium channels or against the acetylcholine (Ach) receptors. Symptoms include:

- Tiredness
- Dysarthria
- Double vision and ptosis
- Droop face
- Drooling
- Weak all limbs
- Head drop
- Nasal voice

Causes: Thymoma (CT thymus to check), Lupus

Investigation: *Edrophonium* (Ach-ase inhibitor) causes the eyes to open back up

Treatment:

Pyridostigmina (Ach-ase inhibitor)

Immunosuppressant (*prednisolone/ Mycophenolate*)

Give D3 + *Alandronic acid* (protect bones from steroid) + *lansoprazole* (PPI)

75

Symptoms include:

- Fatigue
- Vision problems (appears like their eyes are vibrating)
- Muscle spasms, stiffness and weakness
- Mobility problems
- Pain
- Problems with thinking, learning and planning
- Depression and anxiety
- Sexual problems
- Bladder problems
- Bowel problems
- Speech and swallowing difficulties

Caused by the demyelination of the nerve axons from an autoimmune attack of myelin. Accumulation of neurological inflammation causes lesions known as plaques or sclerosis, hence the name 'multiple sclerosis'. Symptoms can relapse and remiss.

Normally the Blood Brain Barrier (BBB) prevents immune cells from entering the brain but in MS they pass between the tight junctions of the endothelial cells and breakdown the basement membrane. The immune cells see myelin as foreign and provoke an immune response, this involves cytokines which cause the BBB to become more permeable to immune cells. Initially oligodendrocytes will myelinate the axons but this will eventually tire and is also at a much slower rate than the degradation taking place.

Investigations and treatment

Visual evoked potential / MRI / Lumbar puncture (for immunoglobulin).

Most treatment is for the relapse and remissive MS and uses immunosuppressants or β-interferons.

Physical therapy for symptomatic control of muscle pain/ numbness/ fatigue

Cognitive rehabilitation therapy

SAH:

- Sudden onset of severe headache (the classic feature)
- Accompanying nausea or vomiting
- Symptoms of meningeal irritation
- Photophobia and visual changes
- Focal neurologic deficits

Investigations = PT time, CT scan. Treatment = Anti-hypertensive agents (e.g., IV beta blockers)

TIA:

Examination include the following:

- Cranial nerve testing
- Somatic motor strength
- Somatic sensory testing
- Speech and language testing
- Assessment of the cerebellar system (be sure to watch the patient walk)

Investigations = A finger stick blood glucose to rule out hypoglycaemia. CT angiogram. Treatment = *Aspirin/Clopidogrel*.

Embolic stroke:

Investigations = CT scan, carotid duplex scan. Treatment = *Alteplase* (fibrinolytic)

EPILEPSY

A transient episode of abnormal neurological function caused by a sudden disturbance in cortical neuronal activity. Usually takes place during childhood or when patients are older than 50 years old (injury from strokes, cancer, old age).

Epileptic seizures:

- Harms self
- Incontinence
- Foaming
- Side Tongue biting
- Head back
- Eyes roll back
- Muscle ache the next day

Psychogenic non-epileptic seizures:

- Harms self
- Sometimes incontinence
- No foam
- Bites tip of tongue
- Varied head movement
- Tremor
- Roll over the room

77

<u>Treatment</u>

If there is any suggestion of alcohol abuse or impaired nutrition, give thiamine as high potency intravenous 'Pabrinex' before glucose, if the cause for the patient's seizure is hypoglycaemia.

Clobazam (acute treatment) / *Carbamazepine* / *Sodium Valproate* / *Phenytoin* / *lamotrigine* / *Topiramate* / vagal nerve stimulation.

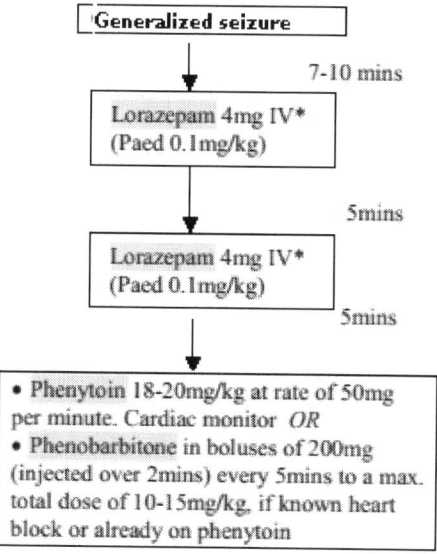

2 main types of seizures:

Focal (partial)	Generalised (both hemispheres)
Simple – remain conscious and aware	Absence (petit mal) – suddenly stop/ repetitive blinking. EEG show normal 3 spike wave at 3hertz
Complex – unaware/unconscious/ blank. Usually has a warning, is periodical, stereotypical behaviours; lip smacking (temporal lobe), swallowing (Autonomic nerves)	Tonic/clonic (grand mal) – stiffening/jerking phase, sudden onset, commonly during sleep
	Myoclonic – jerking, very brief, don't lose awareness, precipitated by alcohol/sleep deprivation
*difference between complex partial and absence = stereotypical behaviour of complex partial is the difference.	Atonic – loss of tone, lose consciousness, drop to the floor, involves all the body, should wear a helmet

<u>Causes of seizures</u>:

Central nervous system: Stroke, trauma, tumour, CNS infection

Systemic: Metabolic, toxins/drug, hypoxia, alcohol withdrawal

Syndromes: Childhood absence epilepsy (remits with puberty, familial, can have fits 100x per day). Juvenile myoclonic epilepsy (presents as absences/jerks in the morning and requires lifelong treatment). Both treated with sodium valproate.

Differential Diagnosis: Syncope, transient ischaemic attack, narcolepsy, cataplexy, amesia, fainting.

FOCAL LIMB WEAKNESS

Request bloods: B_{12}, Thyroid, Glucose, Creatinine kinase. Try to also consider musculoskeletal causes.

SYNCOPE CAUSES

Low Blood pressure:

- Postural hypotension (>20mmhg systole)
- Vaso vagal (bradycardia + postural hypotension)
- Aortic stenosis
- Mituretic hypotension

Pulse:

- Bradycardia (Stokes Adams)
- AV block
- Hypothyroidism

Neurological:
- Epilepsy

A – Appearance, affect B – behaviour C – communications (verbal/non-verbal) D – ideation E – emotion.

AMHP = someone who can conduct an assessment for mental health, determine if the patient can be detained.

Legal hierarchy = nearest relative (male before female)

You cannot detain OH/Drug users under the mental health act

Section 2 = detaining someone for up to 28 days for an assessment, they can also be treated under this section. You must inform the nearest relative of this. Needs to include two section 12 doctors or 1 and a prior acquaintance of the patient

Section 3 = Treatment must be available or the patient cannot be held under this act. Need the approval of the nearest relative to use section 3. Can be used up to 6 months long.

Section 4 = Used rather than a section 2 (when two section 12 doctors are not available). Requires only 1 section 12 doctor. Lasts for 28 days. Should be followed by a section 2 in 72 hours (if staff is available)

Section 5 = Section 5 cannot be used to admit a patient. 5(1) is a nurses holding power for assessment of a patient. 5(2) is a doctors holding power for assessment of a patient up to 72 hours.

Section 17 = 17(E) allows a patient to be discharged into the community. **117** = ensuring the patent has aftercare once discharged

Section 135 = 135(1) is used for house entry for an AMHP. 135(2) is used to remove a patient from their home to hospital.

Viral diarrhoea

Frequent, watery bowel movements, abdominal cramps, and a low-grade fever. Viral diarrhoea generally lasts approximately 3 to 7 days (send stool sample after 7 days)

Bacterial diarrhoea

Bacterial infections also cause severe symptoms, often with vomiting, fever, and severe abdominal cramps or abdominal pain. Bowel movements occur frequently and may be watery and individuals may experience "explosive diarrhoea" which is a very forceful, almost violent, expulsion of loose, watery stool along with gas. Dehydration symptoms may also present.

Check:

- o Recent foreign travel
- o Food poisoning (group of people with similar symptoms)
- o New medications
- o Diet
- o Alcohol
- o Chronic

Rotavirus is common in infants. Norovirus is commonest of all ages. Adenovirus affects all ages.

Treatment

Avoid milk and spicy food. BRAT diet. Avoid strenuous activity (dehydration).Drink plenty of fluids.

Check for blood, tenesmus or any change in bowel habits.

Paracetamol (fever), *Loperamide/Codeine phosphate* (anti-diarrhoeal) but prolongs symptoms.

CONSTIPATION

Check if the patient had constipation with overflow diarrhoea. Check if on opioid medication, dehydrated (older), check coeliac (TTG blood test), check thyroid, and check calcium.

Treatment

Prune/ Pear/ Apple juice

Phosphate enema / Glycine suppository

Causes: -Motion sickness

-GI infection

-Otitis/tonsillitis

-Obstructive

-Acute Abdomen (appendix)

-CNS (vertigo, labrynthitis)

-DKA

-Pregnancy (hyperemesis gravidarum)

-Anorexia

-Alcohol

-Opioids

Management: Take small fluid sips and stay food free for 24hours.

Check for any blood brought up or if there is a Malory-Vice tear.

Remember that posseting is normal in babies

Primary	vs	Secondary
Specific types		Symptom of other conditions
Episodic (5-7d-wk)		Potentially fatal
Modified by drugs		Needs investigation

Ask if anything makes them worse, loss of weight, neurological symptoms, cardiac causes (smoking, diet, exercise, and lifestyle), cardiac history and how much time they have been off from work because of headaches.

Red Flag signs:

- New onset in over 50 years old and under 10 years old
- Personality changes
- Change in headache pattern
- Ptosis (damaged to sympathetic nerves around the carotid/ Carotid dissection/ Tumour)
- Seizures (cortical irritation – structural pathology)
- Fever (Epidural abscess / meningitis)
- Raised ICP symptoms (confusion, nausea +vomiting, tiredness/ stupor)
- Sudden (SAH) CT scan and lumber puncture (>24hrs after) (xanthachroma) check for aneurysms to clip or coil. Treat with oral *Nimodipine*
- Posterior fossa tumour (limbs and balance affected + nausea +vomit)
- Double vision (CN6-horizontal. CN3-vertical) (venous sinus thrombosis)(pituitary tumour)
- Pituitary Apoplexy (Bitemporal hemianopia, CN3 palsy and stiff neck) Treat with *Dexamethasone*

Cluster headache	• Red and watering eye • Drooping and swelling of one eyelid • Unilateral pain, usually by the eye • Sweaty face • Blocked or runny nostril • Red ear • These attacks generally last between 15 minutes and three hours
Trigeminal neuralgia	• Sudden, severe, shocks to jaw/teeth/gums
Cervicogenic headache	• Posterior headache • Radiates to neck and shoulder • Nausea • Photophobia • Constant pain

Investigations: Lumbar puncture:

-Blood (yellow from bilirubin) (SAH)

-Neutrophils (bacterial)

-Lymphocytes (viral) (check TB, Listeria)

-Protein (>ICP)

Treatment

- Migraine = *Aspirin/Ibuprofen* + anti-emetic , *Sumatriptan/Zolmitriptan*
- Cluster = Oxygen, *Zolmitriptan*, intranasal lidocaine
- Trigeminal = *Carbamazepine/Gabapentin*
- Cervicogenic = Great occipital nerve block, *Amitriptyline/Gabapentin*
- Tension = Reduce stress/*Amitriptyline*

Acute = Meningitis, Encephalitis, SAH, Injury, Sinusitis, Dental, Tropical illness

Subacute = Temporal arteritis (Check ESR)

Chronic = Tension, Cervicogenic, Medication over-use

Recurrent = Migraine, Cluster, Exertional, Coital, Trigeminal neuralgia, Cervicogenic, Glaucoma (will also have visual disturbance)

BACK PAIN

Age 15-30 years = Postural, Prolapse, Mechanical, Trauma, Ankylosing spondylosis, Spondylolisthesis, Sciatica, Pregnancy.

Age 50 years or older = Osteoporosis, Myeloma, Referred pain.

Cauda equina	Fracture	Cancer
• <20yr >50yr	• sudden pain relieved laying down	• pain when laying
• Bowel/Bladder	• point tenderness	• history of Ca
• Dysfunction	• heavy lifting/trauma	• fever/chills
• Neurological deficit		• weight loss
• Saddle anaesthesia		

Investigations: ESR, FBC, ALP (Paget's disease)

Treatment: Physiotherapy / Analgesia / Heat / Calcium phosphate

MUSCLE PAIN

Quinine (Muscle cramps/preventative)

Methocarbamol (Acute spasm)

Baclofen (Chronic spasm)

5 I's of elderly medicine:

- Instability
- Immobility
- Incontinence
- Impaired memory
- Iatrogenic disease/polypharmacy

Always check whether or not a patient needs all the medication they're on.

Temperature: older patients do not always have a physiological response to illness so may present with no fever

Blood Pressure: higher resting systolic and lower diastolic (>pulse pressure), most are hypertensive therefore there is often a postural drop

Cardiac system: Murmurs are more common from calcification, as well as bradycardia, heart blocks and AF

Respiratory system: Kyphosis results in restricted breathing, around 30% have basal creps asymptomatic

Gastrointestinal: Majority are constipated (check >ca), poor dental health

Urogenital: Many have asymptomatic UTI's, always check if retention is due to constipation

Central nervous system: Poorer sensation in feet

Investigations: ESR rises with age, more false positive ANA/d-Dimer/Troponin

Make problem list for geriatric patients, if memory issues ask collateral history 'when was their memory as good as yours?'

May be generally unwell with no obvious cause. Urinary tract is normal in most with UTI-35% will have vesico-ureteric reflux.

Any paediatric age with recurrent infection should be investigated with:

-USS (URGENT if less than 6 months old)

-DMSA scan

-MCUG if less than 6 months old

<u>Treatment</u>

Fluids (3 Litres /24hrs), Oral Antibiotics-check for local resistance

- *Trimethoprim* (3 days for Lower UTI, 7-10days for Upper UTI)
- *Ciprofloxacin* (Pyelonephritis)
- *Ciprofloxacin/Trimethoprim* (Prostatitis)

Balanitis, or balanoposthitis, is inflammation of the head of the penis.

- Redness, swelling and soreness around the head of the penis or foreskin
- Thick discharge under the foreskin
- Rashes on the penis
- Itchiness
- Unpleasant odour
- Pain when urinating

It can be caused by skin conditions such as Lichen Planus, bacterial infection, sexually transmitted infections, after soap use or antibiotic use.

<u>Treatment</u>

Corticosteroids/ Antibiotics/ Antifungals

PAEDS: HYPOSPADIUS

Hypospadias is a congenital abnormality of anterior urethral and penile development in which the urethral opening is ectopically located on the ventral aspect of the penis.

Treatment is surgery.

PAEDS: NOCTURNAL ENURESIS

Family members with a history of enuresis should be encouraged to share their experiences and offer moral support to the child. The knowledge that another family member had and outgrew the problem can be helpful. Initial management focusing on behavioural modification and positive reinforcement.

Patients with enuresis should keep a diary and should return for evaluation on a monthly basis to assess their progress. Keeping a normal daytime pattern is important but if after 3 months this does not result in dryness, then either alarm therapy or pharmacologic therapy should be considered.

Bedwetting alarms can be difficult if the parents share a room with the child.

Medication: *Desmopressin* just before bed/ *Oxybutynin* (side effects of constipation/diarrhoea)/ *Imipramine* (relaxes bladder to allow it to store more).

PAEDS: HAEMOLYTIC URAEMIC SYNDROME

- Several days of diarrhoea
- With or without vomiting
- Irritability
- Pallor
- Diarrhoea can be visibly bloody
- Oedema
- Thrombocytopenia

Acute kidney injury usually begins with the onset of haemolytic anaemia.

The hallmark of haemolytic uremic syndrome in the peripheral smear is the presence of schistocytes. These consist of fragmented, deformed, irregular, or helmet-shaped red blood cells.

Treatment

Ciprofloxacin /Azathioprine as this is most often caused by E.coli 0157.

In babies it can be quite normal to bring up food and they soon grow out of it after a few months. The symptoms of gastroesophageal reflux are most often directly related to the consequences of poor weight gain. The typical adult symptoms (e.g., heartburn, vomiting, and regurgitation) cannot be readily assessed in infants and children. Instead, in babies looks for:

- Vomiting
- Wheezing
- Check teeth for dental problems (acid)

Diagnosed by barium contrast of gastroesophageal space.

Treatment

Small frequent feeds, avoid citrus foods, caffeine, alcohol and smoking (teenagers)

Antacids / H_2 / Proton pump inhibitor

An acute infection of the bronchioles that is usually caused by a viral infection (most commonly respiratory syncytial virus). Children may become increasingly fussy and have difficulty feeding during the 2 to 5 day incubation period. It can cause wheeze and around 1/3 develop a lower chest infection.

- Low-grade fever, possible hypothermia if younger than 1 month old
- Increasing coryza and congestion
- Apnoea
- Respiratory distress with tachypnoea and intercostal recession
- Irritability
- Possibly cyanosis

Investigations and treatment

Nasopharyngeal aspirate / X-ray. O_2 and hydration or usually supportive care is usually sufficient but if not then consider antivirals and corticosteroids.

Viral = 7-10 day duration in children

If symptoms last longer than 2 weeks, consider alternative diagnoses, such as allergy, sinusitis, mononucleosis, tuberculosis, or pneumonia.

Symptoms:

- Rhinorrhoea
- Sore throat
- Cough (post nasal drip)
- Sinus symptoms
- Fever
- Nausea/vomiting/diarrhoea/abdomen pain
- Absence of cough and rhinorrhoea suggests group A strep (rheumatic fever)

Bacterial symptoms:

- Persistent nasal discharge (any type) or cough lasting 10 days or more without improvement
- Worsening course
- 3 consecutive days of fever

PAEDS: EPIGLOTTITIS

This condition is more often found in children aged 1-5 years old, who present with a sudden onset of the following symptoms:

- Sore throat
- Drooling
- dysphagia and globus
- Muffled or loss of voice
- Dry cough
- Fever
- Tripod or sniffing posture

Do not try to visualise the area as there is a risk of laryngospasm. Seek anaesthetic assistance.

Viral: Nasopharyngitis often precedes croup, swallowing may be difficult or painful, and patients may experience a globus sensation.

Children with laryngotracheitis (croup) may have the characteristic seal-like barking cough. Symptoms may be worse at night.

Tends to present around winter time. There is no need for antibiotics and it can be treated with humidified air and steroids. Croup responds well to steroids, such as oral *dexamethasone*, *prednisolone* or nebulised *budesonide*. In severe croup, an adrenaline nebuliser can be used for a more immediate effect.

Bordetella pertussis is a bacterial infection. In whooping cough, the classic whoop sound is an inspiratory gasping squeak typically between coughs. The whoop is more common in children. Coughing often comes in waves of several coughs or more at a time and is often worst at night.

Whooping cough has 3 classic phases:

- Catarrhal (1 week): With predominantly URI symptoms
- Paroxysmal (1-6 weeks): With episodic cough
- Convalescent (1 week): Gradual recovery

Vomiting and subconjunctival haemorrhage may result from severe cough. Rib pain with pinpoint tenderness worsening with respiration may suggest rib fractures associated with the coughing.

Tracheal tug and intercostal recessions may be present in patients with severe whooping cough. Apnoea may be a main feature in infants with pertussis. It is a self-limiting condition.

Individuals with acute tonsillitis present with the following:

- Fever
- Sore throat
- Foul breath
- Dysphagia (difficulty swallowing)
- Odynophagia (painful swallowing)
- Tender cervical lymph nodes (check if Glandular fever (Full blood count + Paul Bunnell/Monospot test) and palpate spleen for enlargement)

Airway obstruction may present as mouth breathing, snoring, sleep-disordered breathing, and sleep apnoea. Most cases are viral or caused by group A streptococcus pyogenes.

Tonsillitis is scored according to a Centor Score: C - Cough absent, T – Transudates, N – Nodes, T - temperature (fever), OR - young OR old modifier. Scores of 2-3 requires a swab. 4-5 requires rapid strep test.

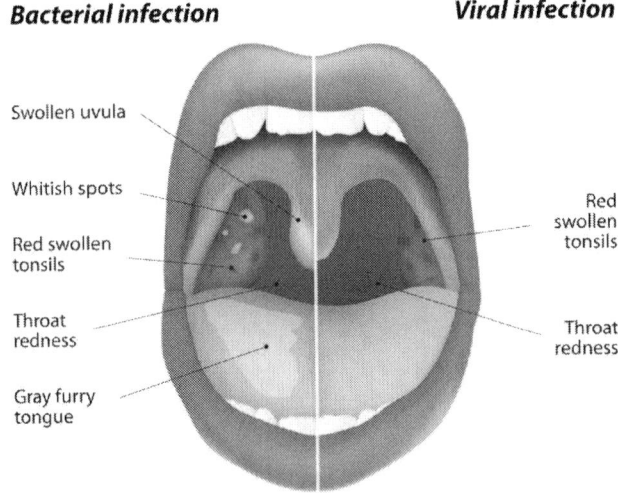

Individuals with peritonsillar abscess (PTA) present with the following:

- Severe throat pain
- Fever
- Drooling
- Foul breath
- Trismus (difficulty opening the mouth)
- Altered voice quality (the hot-potato voice)

Physical examination of a PTA almost always reveals unilateral bulging above and lateral to one of the tonsils.

Treatment of acute tonsillitis is largely supportive and focuses on maintaining adequate hydration and food intake, controlling pain and fever. *Benzydamine* spray (numbs throat) or *Codeine* pain relief.

Tonsillectomy is indicated for the individuals who have experienced the following:

- More than six episodes in 1 year

Treatment of PTA: Antibiotic coverage or incision and drainage (I&D). Antibiotics, either orally or intravenously are required to treat PTA.

PAEDS: BLOOD PRESSURE

Age (years)	Systolic blood pressure
<1	70-90
1-2	80-95
2-5	80-100
5-12	90-110
>12	100-120

PAEDS: DIABETES

Blood glucose <2.6mmol = hypoglycaemia

>7mmol (fasting) or >11mmol (random) = hyperglycaemia (diabetes)

Symptoms:

Hyperglycaemia, malaise, headaches, and weakness. Children may also appear irritable and become ill-tempered. Children may get nocturia and weight loss despite usual eating habits. They may also be tachycardic and have blurred vision.

Investigation

Urine dip & blood glucose

Treatment

Exercise and diet and to make parents aware of signs of hypoglycaemia. It is also important to train parents to use the subcutaneous injections for insulin. Another important factor is illness, parents need to be made to aware that during sick days children will require more insulin because of the body's release of cortisol during infections which oppose the action of insulin.

Review at least once annually to examine the patient for possible complications. Examination and review should include a growth assessment as well as screening for thyroid disorders and coeliac disease.

For hypoglycaemia:

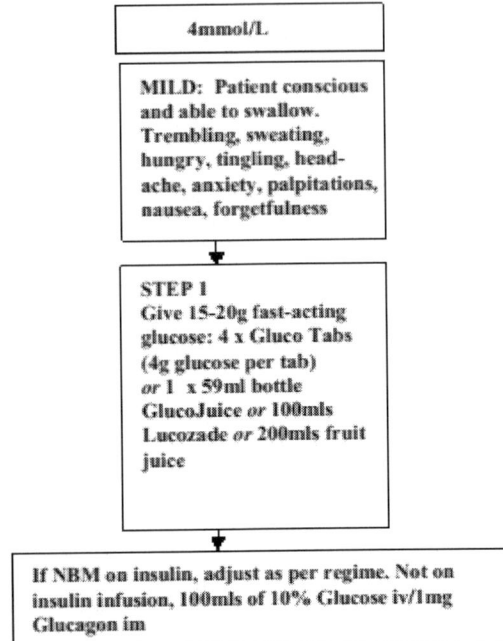

Diabetic ketoacidosis

Symptoms:

- Severe dehydration
- Smell of ketones
- Acidotic breathing (Kussmaul respiration)
- Abdominal pain
- Vomiting
- Drowsiness and coma

<u>Investigations</u>
Urine dip, HbA1C, U+E's (check for renal damage), ABG, blood glucose and blood ketones (normal ketones range is 0.6-3).

<u>Treatment</u>
Fluid bolus (20ml/kg) to correct dehydration from high circulating glucose.
Insulin is started about an hour later, this is because if insulin is administered too soon then it will not only draw in the glucose back into cells but also:

1. Potassium
2. Water

This can result in a patient late during treatment getting a hypokalaemia or cerebral oedema from water retention. A way to identify if cerebral oedema may be occurring is to monitor the patient to see if the heart rate is dropping and the blood pressure rising. In addition to this, neurological examinations should be done hourly as well as ABG and U&E's to monitor potassium.

Normally around 0.5 units of insulin/kg/day is used.

PAEDS: HYPOTHYROIDISM

Earliest signs of hypothyroidism:

- Prolonged pregnancy
- High birth weight
- Delayed stool after birth
- Jaundice
- Poor feeding
- Hypothermia
- Decreased activity
- Hoarse cry
- Delayed bone maturation
- Testicular enlargement in boys or early breast development or vaginal bleeding in girls

- Pain in the abdomen or at right iliac fossa
- Fever.
- Nausea and/or diarrhoea.
- May have had a sore throat or flu symptoms prior to abdominal pain

Usually resolves on its own (viral infection).

ENT and Ophthalmology

Ask:

1. SOCRATES method of assessing any pain
2. Watery?
3. Sore?
4. Dry?
5. Visual acuity, Partial loss?
6. Flashing lights?
7. Fever? Runny nose? Sore throat? Cough?
8. Headache?
9. Ear pain?
10. Photophobia?

PMH: Cataract surgery (Endophthalmitis)

- Retinal detachment is more common in short sighted people

-Glaucoma acute closure angle is common in long sighted people

- HTN, Sjogrens, SLE, Thyroid eye etc.

FH: Glaucoma (blindness over many years)

Albinism (no iris/ no fovea)

Retinitis pigmentation

DH and Allergies: TB drugs, Topiramate

SH: Smoke/OH

Job (cleaners, wielders)

Sexual: Chlamydia (red watery eye)

Systemic: Ankylosing spondylosis (Uveitis)

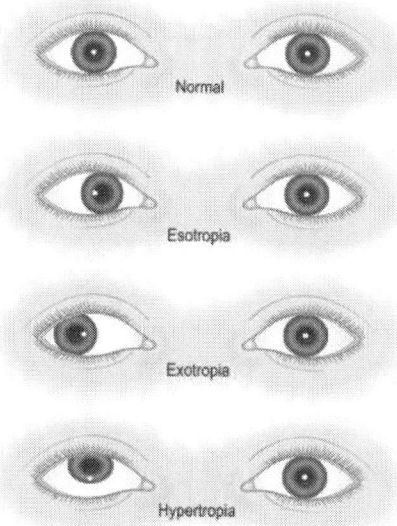

If the eyes rest in a down and out position, with dilated pupil = cranial nerve III palsy which can be caused by a posterior communicating artery aneurysm.

Muscles = oblique's are medial, rectus are lateral

If the eye cannot move laterally = cranial nerve VI lesion.

If the eye cannot move inferiorly medially = cranial nerve IV lesion.

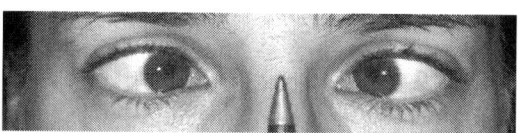

Convergence test: Pupils should constrict and eyes should converge as shown.

Can be the normal reaction in around 20% of the population.

Tested in	Dim light	Bright light
Positive sign =	Does not dilate	Does not constrict

AFFERENT PATHWAY DEFECT

Test each eye individually. When there is a defect in one of the optic nerves it will dilate in response to direct light and cause a consensual dilation in the other, healthy eye. Furthermore when light is directed in the healthy eye it will constrict and cause consensual constriction of the eye with an afferent pathway defect.

ADIES

Large pupils, absent light reflex, slow pupil constriction, vermiform movements, and diminished tendon reflexes. Often in females or post-viral infections.

Treatment

Pilocarpine (abnormal pupil will constrict)

HORNER'S

Ptosis, Miosis, Anhydrosis, Enophthalamos (sunken eyes), and the Ciliospinal reflex is also lost (normally pain causes eye constriction)

Causes

- Lesion of the primary neuron
- Brainstem stroke or tumour or syrinx of the preganglionic neuron
- Trauma to the brachial plexus
- Tumours (e.g. Pancoast tumour) or infection of the lung apex
- Lesion of the postganglionic neuron
- Dissecting carotid aneurysm /internal carotid artery dissections
- Carotid artery ischemia
- Migraine
- Middle cranial fossa neoplasm

Treatment

Treat the cause / Alpha agonist (*Apraclonidine*) dilates Horner's eye.

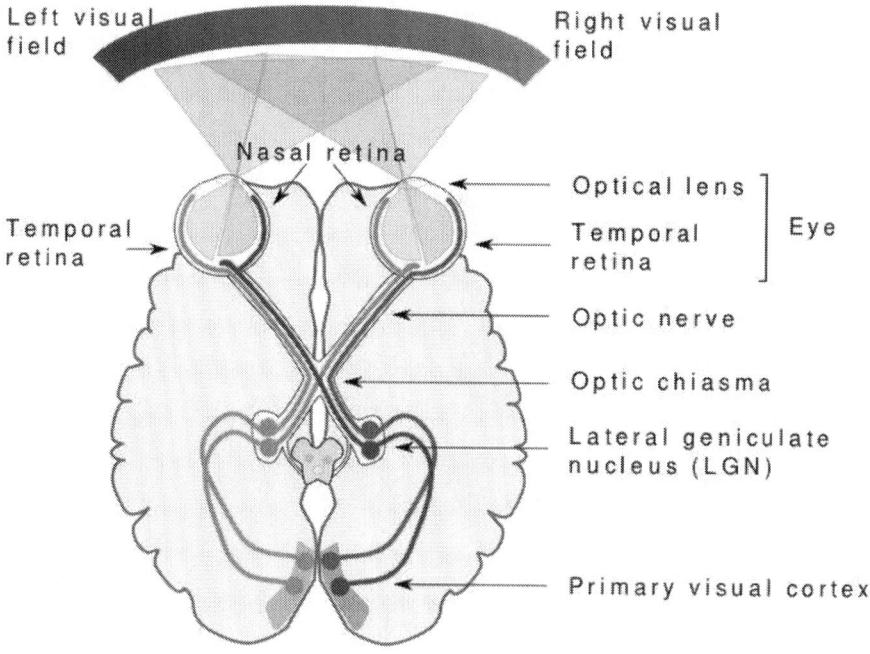

Left visual field

Right visual field

Nasal retina

Temporal retina

Optical lens ⎤
Temporal retina ⎥ Eye
⎦

Optic nerve

Optic chiasma

Lateral geniculate nucleus (LGN)

Primary visual cortex

Tested at arm's length, ask if they can see the whole of your face. Cover one eye at a time and test visual fields, also ask if they can see your face with that eye covered.

Describe: colour, cup/ratio, and shape (blurred etc.)

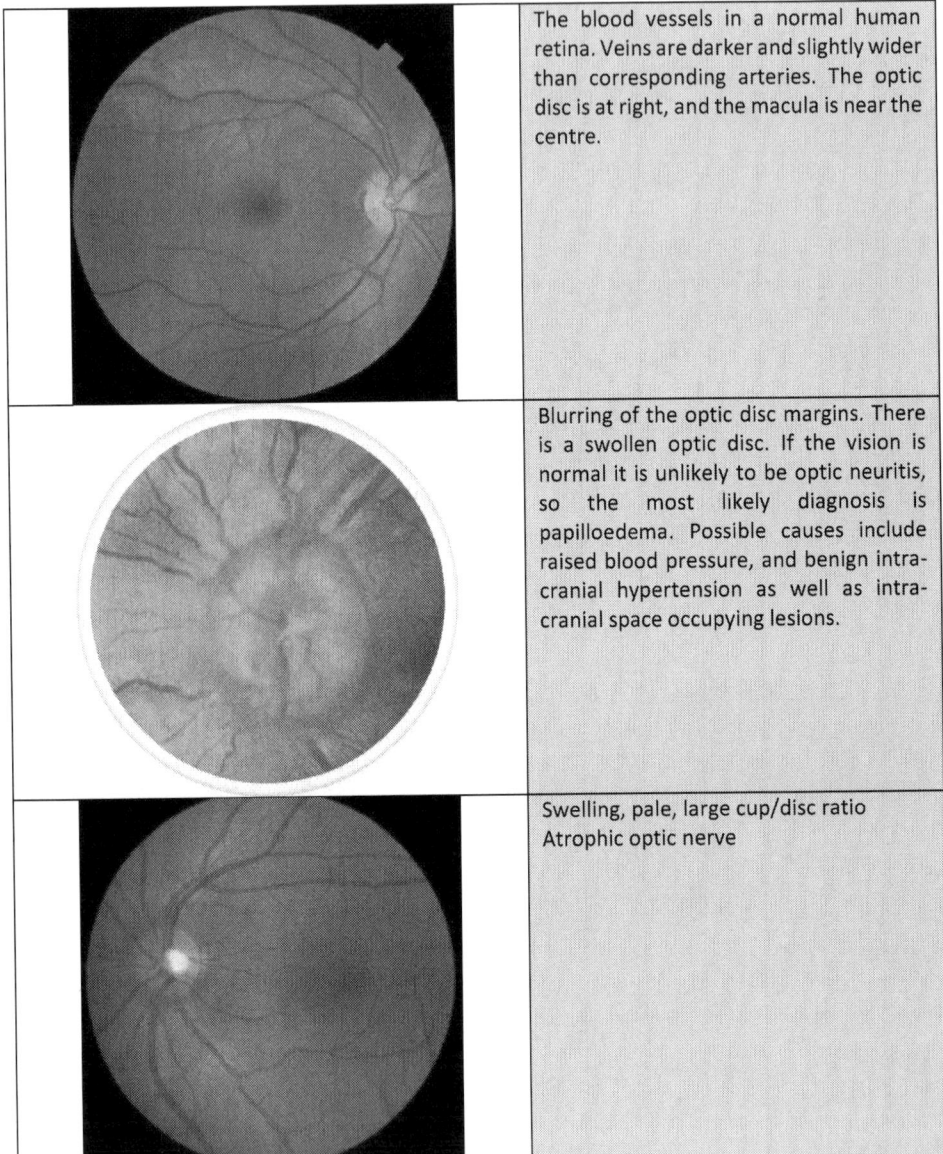

	The blood vessels in a normal human retina. Veins are darker and slightly wider than corresponding arteries. The optic disc is at right, and the macula is near the centre.
	Blurring of the optic disc margins. There is a swollen optic disc. If the vision is normal it is unlikely to be optic neuritis, so the most likely diagnosis is papilloedema. Possible causes include raised blood pressure, and benign intra-cranial hypertension as well as intra-cranial space occupying lesions.
	Swelling, pale, large cup/disc ratio Atrophic optic nerve

		Cup/ disc ratio is enlarged. Optic nerve in glaucoma
		Retinal detachment. The wrinkled surface of the retina, and the loss of the normal red reflex are characteristic of a retinal detachment. The flashes and floaters are common symptoms. The macula is already detached, but surgery to re-attach the retina will at least restore navigational vision.
		The large number of haemorrhages, the white cotton wool spot, and the poor vision all suggest that this is probably an ischaemic vein occlusion. There is a high risk that this will progress to glaucoma within the next three months. If iris new vessels are detected, then pan-retinal laser can prevent secondary glaucoma.
		Retinal blood vessels pass under the macula. The dark area is due to haemorrhage. Fibrous and vascular tissue has grown from the choroid under the retina at the macula, destroying the photoreceptors at the fovea, and causing irreversible blindness. This is age related macular degeneration.

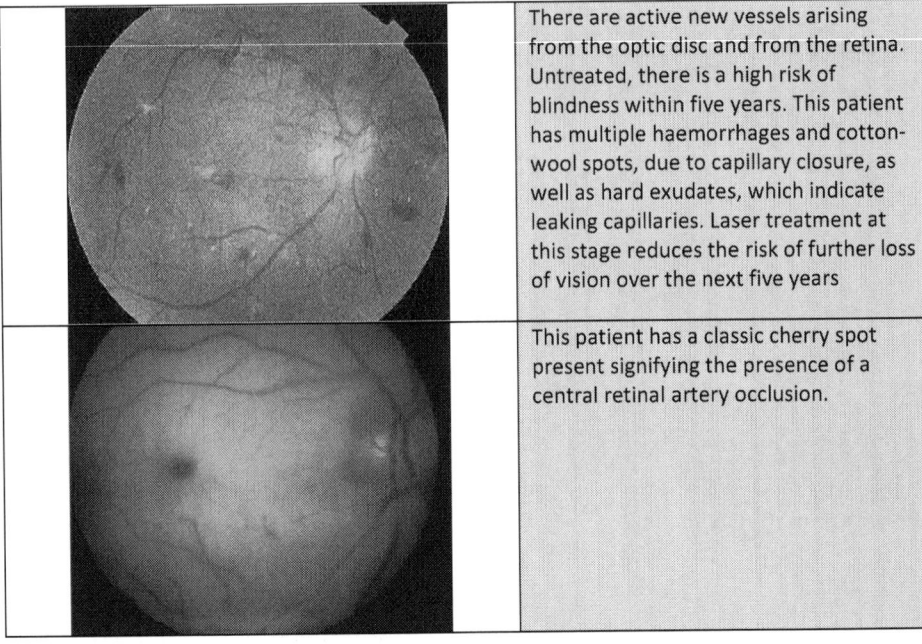

| | There are active new vessels arising from the optic disc and from the retina. Untreated, there is a high risk of blindness within five years. This patient has multiple haemorrhages and cotton-wool spots, due to capillary closure, as well as hard exudates, which indicate leaking capillaries. Laser treatment at this stage reduces the risk of further loss of vision over the next five years |
| | This patient has a classic cherry spot present signifying the presence of a central retinal artery occlusion. |

BLEPHARITIS

Family of inflammatory disease processes of the eyelid(s). Blepharitis can be divided anatomically into anterior and posterior blepharitis. Anterior blepharitis refers to inflammation mainly centred around the skin, eyelashes, and lash follicles, while the posterior involves the Meibomian glands. Frequently, it involves bacterial colonization of the eyelids. Symptoms:

- Burning
- Watering
- Foreign body sensation
- Crusting and mattering of the lashes and medial canthus
- Red lids
- Red eyes
- Photophobia
- Pain

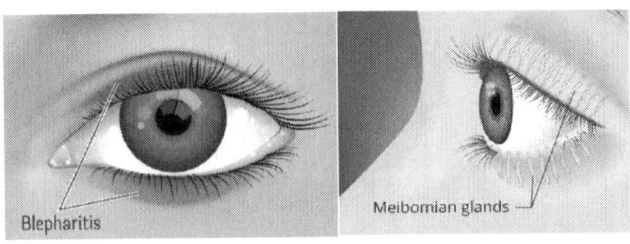

Treatment

Warm water in a washcloth / *Bacitracin* / *Polymyxin B* / *Erythromycin* / *Sulfacetamide* ointments / Artificial tear solutions (*hypromellous*).

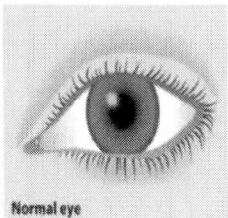 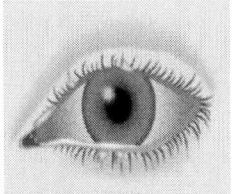 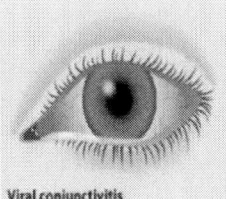 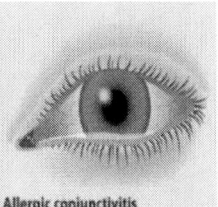

Normal eye   Bacterial conjunctivitis   Viral conjunctivitis   Allergic conjunctivitis

- Enlarged pre-auricular lymph node: Common in viral conjunctivitis and unusual in bacterial conjunctivitis, although found in severe bacterial conjunctivitis caused by *N gonorrhoeae*
- Eyelid oedema: Often present in bacterial conjunctivitis, but mild in most cases. Severe eyelid oedema in the presence of copious purulent discharge raises the suspicion of *N gonorrhoeae* infection.

Viral conjunctivitis- Watery, itchy eyes and sensitivity to light. One or both eyes can be affected and patients may have flu symptoms and pre-auricular lymph involvement. It is highly contagious, can be spread by coughing, sneezing or transmitted from contact lenses and in swimming pools. Usually though this infection is self-limiting and therefore does not require treatment.

Bacterial conjunctivitis- A sticky, yellow or greenish-yellow eye discharge in the corner of the eye. In some cases, this discharge can be severe enough to cause the eyelids to be stuck together when you wake up. One or both eyes can be affected and it is usually spread by direct contact with infected hands or items that have touched the eye.

Treatment

Broad-spectrum agents e.g. *Trimethoprim* with *polymyxin B* / *Azithromycin*

Allergic conjunctivitis- Watery, burning, itchy eyes often accompanied by a blocked or runny nose, and light sensitivity. Both eyes are affected but this is not contagious.

Treatment

Antihistamines

Treated with *Chloramphenicol* (antibacterial). Fluoroquinolones are used commonly in treatment.

KERATITIS

Rapid progressive corneal destruction which may be complete in 24 to 48 hours with some of the more virulent bacteria. Symptoms:

- Ulceration of the epithelium begins with corneal infiltrate with no significant tissue loss to dense, stromal inflammation with indistinct edges to lastly suffering stromal tissue loss and surrounding stromal oedema
- Increased anterior chamber redness
- Folds in the descemet membrane
- Upper eyelid oedema

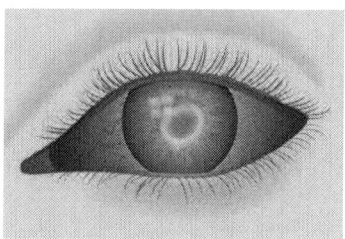

Treatment:

Broad-spectrum antibiotics with the following: *tobramycin* (14 mg/mL) 1 drop every hour alternating with fortified *cefazolin* (50 mg/mL) 1 drop every hour.

PTERYGIUM

An elevated, superficial, external ocular mass that usually forms over the peri-limbal conjunctiva and extends onto the corneal surface.

Presents with no symptoms to significant redness, swelling, itching, irritation, and blurring of vision. Associated with elevated lesions on the conjunctiva in one or both eyes.

Risk factors for pterygium include increased exposure to ultraviolet light, including living in subtropical and tropical climates.

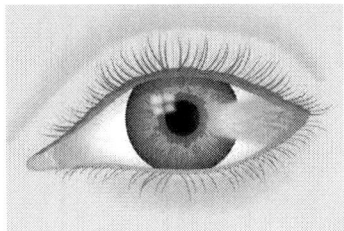

This does not require treatment but can be done for cosmetic reasons.

CHALAZION

CHALAZION

A chalazion usually presents as a painless swelling on the eyelid that has been present for weeks to months.

Symptoms can include eye pain, acute visual changes, recurrence in the same location, fever, limited extraocular movement, and diffuse eyelid or facial swelling.

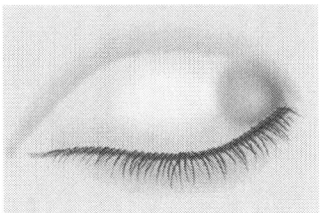

Treatment

Regularly apply a warm, moist compress on the outside of your closed eyelid to promote drainage from the eye's blocked oil gland.

DACROCYSTITIS

Lacrimal excretory system is prone to infection and inflammation. Acquired dacryocystitis can be acute or chronic. Acute dacryocystitis is characterised by the sudden onset of pain and redness in the medial canthal region. The onset of tears is characteristic of chronic inflammation or infection of the lacrimal sac.

Tearing is the most common presentation of chronic dacryocystitis and is related to the obstruction of the tear duct system.

Treatment

Oral antibiotics e.g. *Amoxicillin*

Ectropion is an abnormal eversion of the lid margin away from the eye. Without normal eyelid apposition, corneal exposure, tearing, keratinization of the palpebral conjunctiva, and visual loss may result.

Patients often complain of irritated or red eyes with tearing. They may constantly wipe their eyes, thereby exacerbating lid laxity and the ectropion.

Old age and facial nerve palsy can cause ectropion. Acute facial nerve palsy is consistent with Bell palsy. Chronic, progressive facial nerve palsy may indicate a mass lesion. A history of facial burns, lid surgery, or lid trauma may suggest ectropion.

Treatment

Patients with tearing and ectropion should be instructed to gently wipe the eyelids in a direction up and in (toward the nose) to avoid worsening medial ectropion. Surgery is the cure.

ENTROPION

Entropion is a malposition resulting in inversion of the eyelid margin.

Treatment

Hygiene control and refer to surgery

GLAUCOMA

Symptoms:

- Hazy cornea
- Halos
- Semi dilated pupil
- Painful
- Hard eye (pressure)

The two major categories of glaucoma are open-angle glaucoma (OAG) and narrow angle glaucoma. The "angle" in both cases refers to the drainage angle inside the eye that controls the outflow of the watery fluid that is continually being produced inside the eye.

Open angle glaucoma causes vision loss from the periphery that slowly moves centrally.

Closed-angle or narrow-angle glaucoma produces symptoms such as eye pain, headaches, halos around lights, dilated pupils, vision loss, red eyes, nausea and vomiting.

Treatment: Prostaglandin used in eye drops only once daily. Prostaglandins generally work by relaxing muscles in the eye's interior structure to allow better outflow of fluids, thus reducing build-up of eye pressure.

Beta blockers or carbonic anhydrase inhibitor eye drops can also be used.

BLOW OUT FRACTURE

The inferior rectus muscle or orbital tissue can become entrapped within the fracture, resulting in tethering and restriction of gaze and diplopia

Symptoms:

- Decreased visual acuity
- Blepharoptosis
- Binocular vertical or oblique diplopia (especially in upward gaze)
- Ipsilateral paraesthesia in the distribution of the infraorbital nerve.
- In addition, patients may complain of epistaxis and eyelid swelling following nose blowing

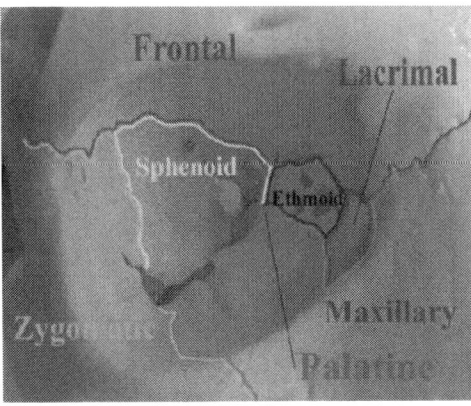

The patient can be treated with oral antibiotics and a short course of oral *prednisone* reduce oedema. Do not give nasal oxygen and avoid blowing the nose to keep pressures low.

Thyroid eye disease is an autoimmune disease affecting ocular and orbital tissues. Symptoms include:

- Dry eyes
- Puffy eyelids
- Angry-looking eyes
- Bulging eyes
- Diplopia
- Visual loss
- Field loss
- Partial colour vision loss
- Photopia on upward gaze
- Ocular pressure or pain

Treatment

Artificial tears / Systemic steroids for severe inflammation.

SUBCONJUNCTIVAL HAEMORRHAGE

Blood between conjunctiva and cornea. No need for referral. Usually resolves by itself.

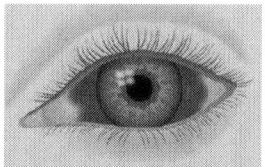

HYPHEMA

Needs referral to ophthalmology. Presence of a blood fluid level line in aqueous humor.

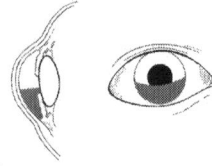

Acute anterior uveitis presents with:

- Pain, generally developing over a few hours or days except in cases of trauma
- Redness
- Photophobia
- Blurred vision
- Increased tears
- Irregular pupil size

Posterior uveitis presents with:

- Blurred vision and floaters

Causes: Autoimmune, Trauma, Viral Conjunctivitis, Ankylosing spondylitis, Herpes, Sarcoidosis and Lyme disease.

Treatment

Check intraocular pressure and rule out herpes simplex virus (HSV) keratitis before starting topical corticosteroids. Initiate steroid treatment only in consultation with an ophthalmologist

Gonococcal conjunctivitis tends to occur 2-7 days after birth but can present later. The onset of chlamydial conjunctivitis is usually after of 5-14 days.

Gonococcal = Severe bilateral purulent conjunctivitis, diffuse opacification, oedema, systemic illness (rhinitis, stomatitis)

Chlamydial = Mild hyperaemia (superficial blood vessels) with mucoid discharge to eyelid swelling, chemosis, and pseudomembrane formation, systemic illness.

Topical *Erythromycin* ointment. Chlamydial conjunctivitis requires systemic treatment because of the significant risk for life-threatening pneumonia.

EARS

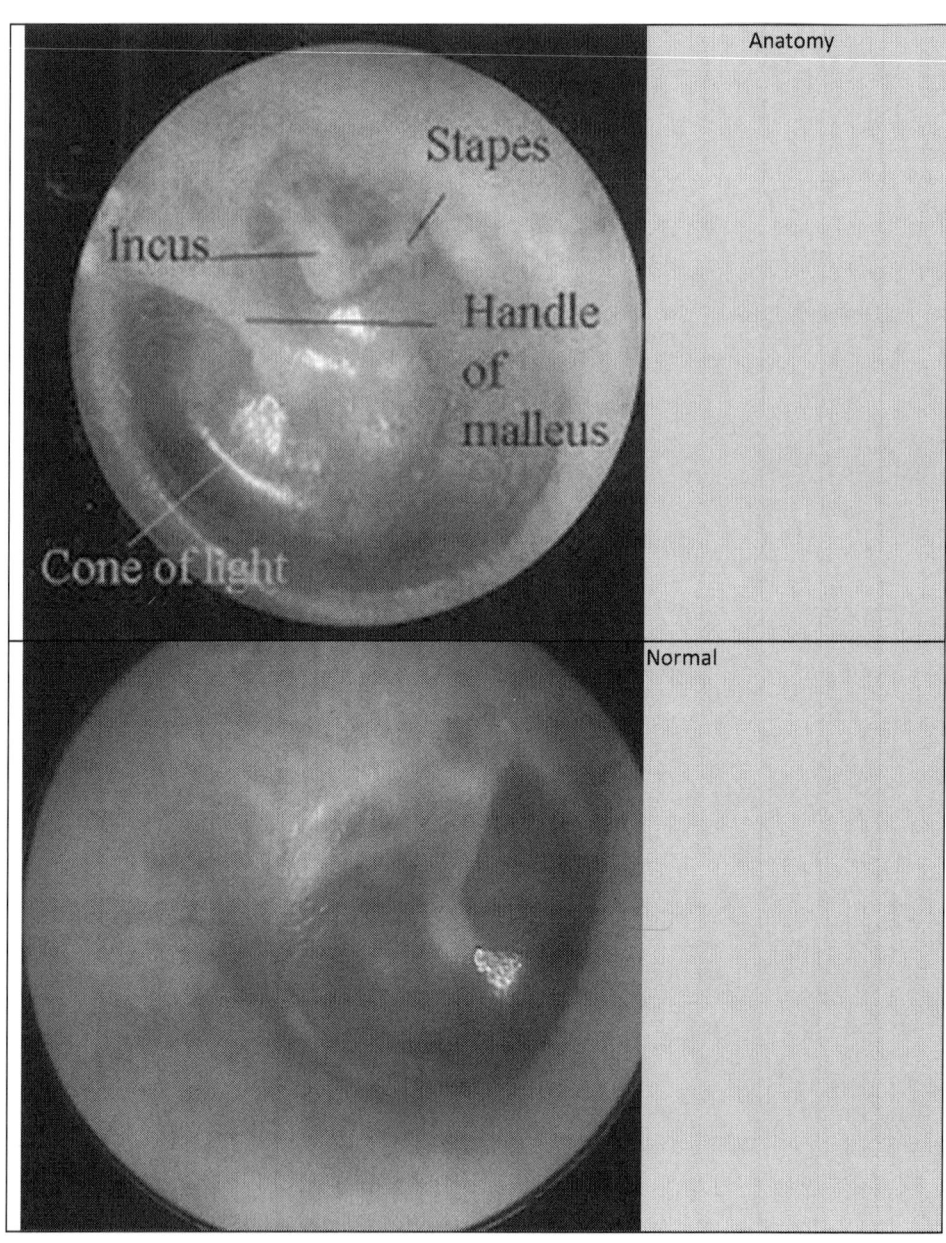

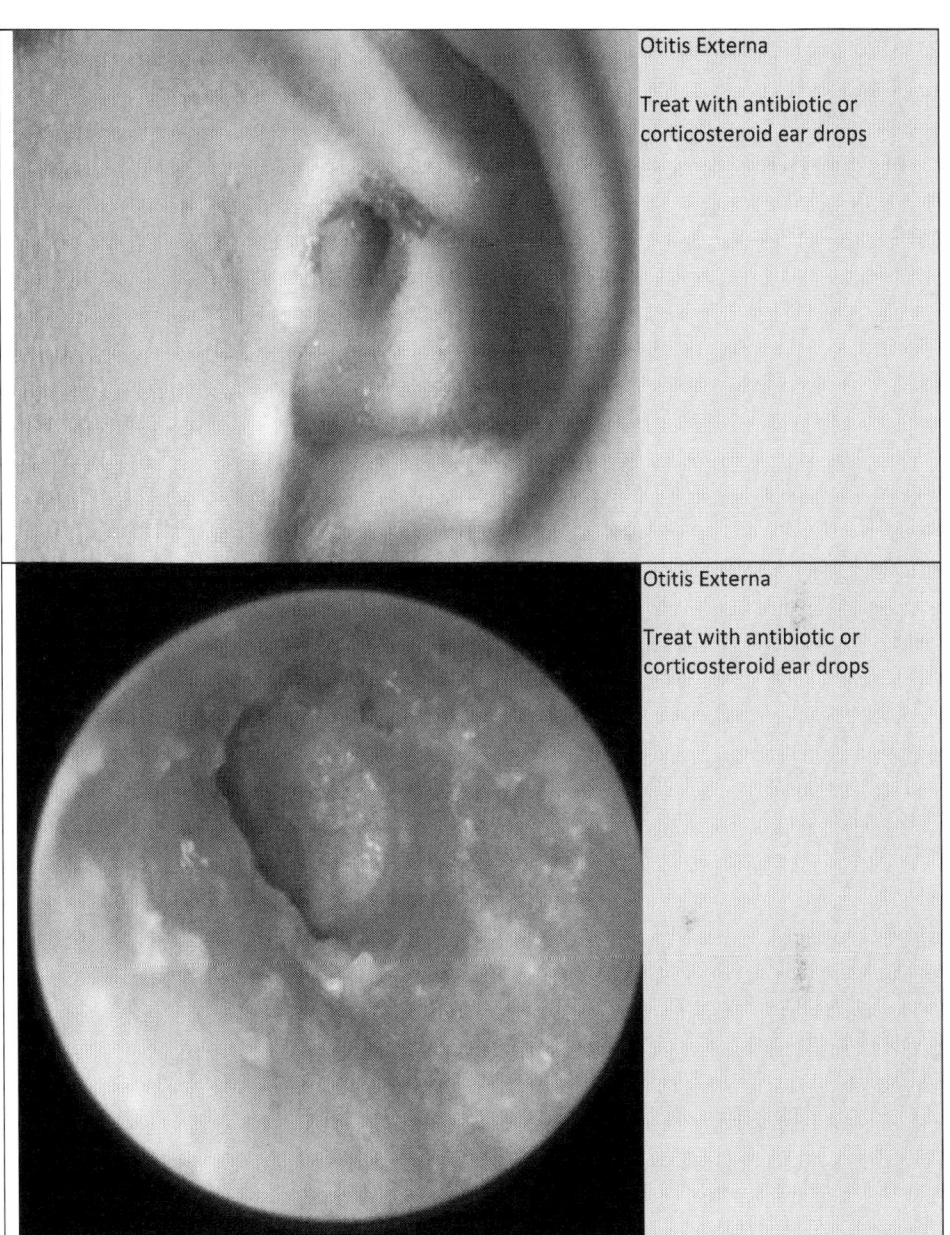

Otitis Externa

Treat with antibiotic or corticosteroid ear drops

Otitis Externa

Treat with antibiotic or corticosteroid ear drops

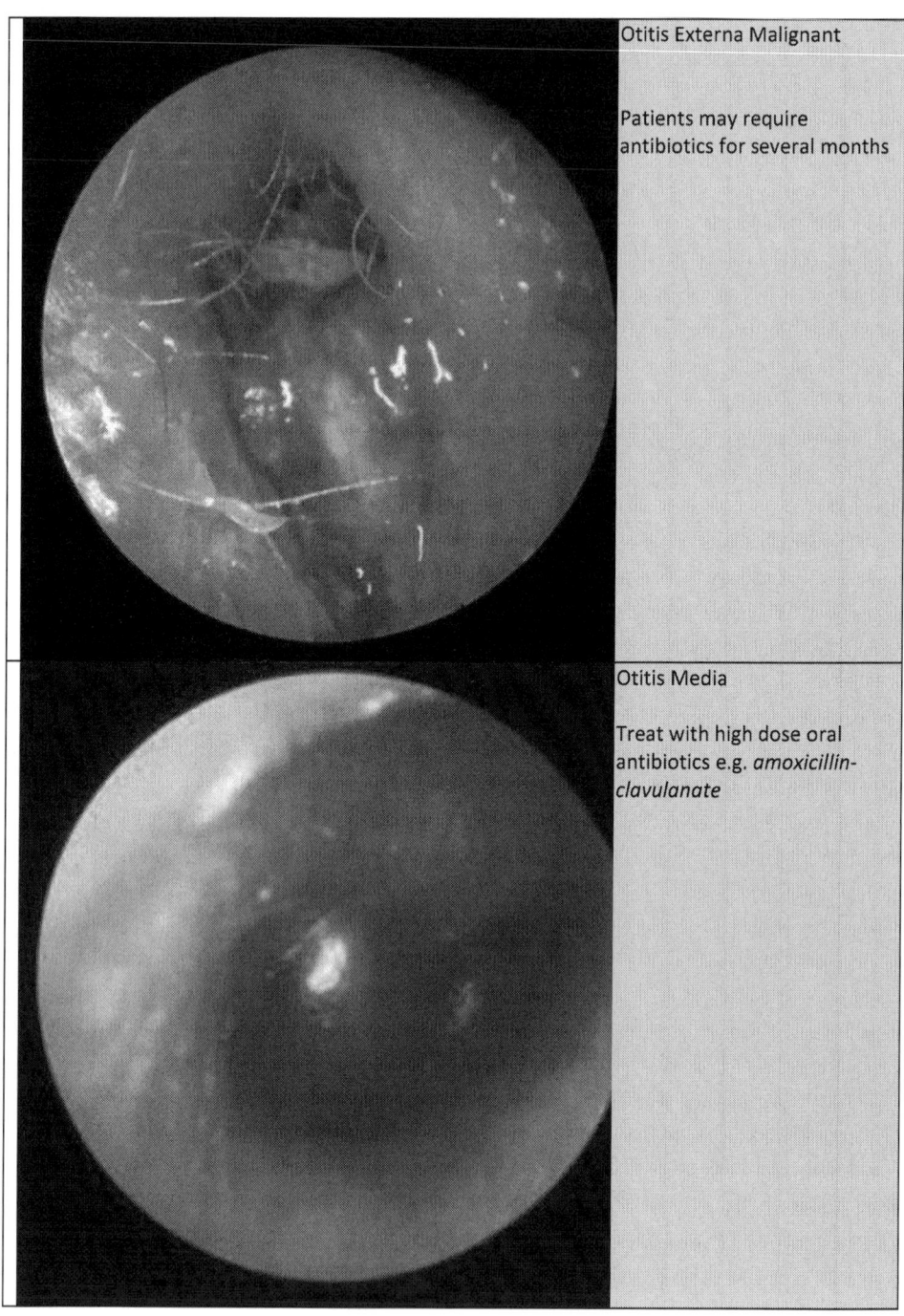

Otitis Externa Malignant

Patients may require antibiotics for several months

Otitis Media

Treat with high dose oral antibiotics e.g. *amoxicillin-clavulanate*

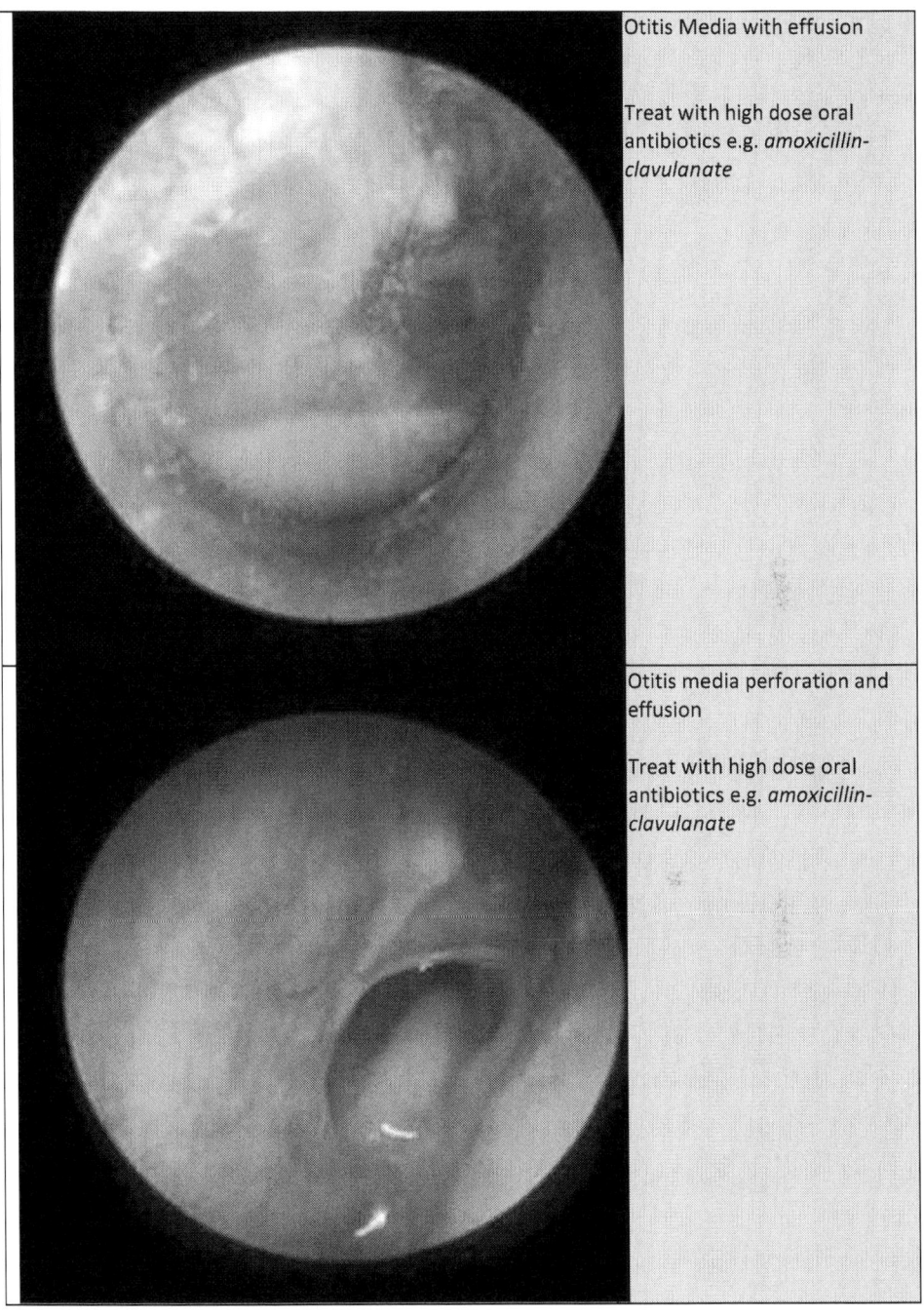

Otitis Media with effusion

Treat with high dose oral antibiotics e.g. *amoxicillin-clavulanate*

Otitis media perforation and effusion

Treat with high dose oral antibiotics e.g. *amoxicillin-clavulanate*

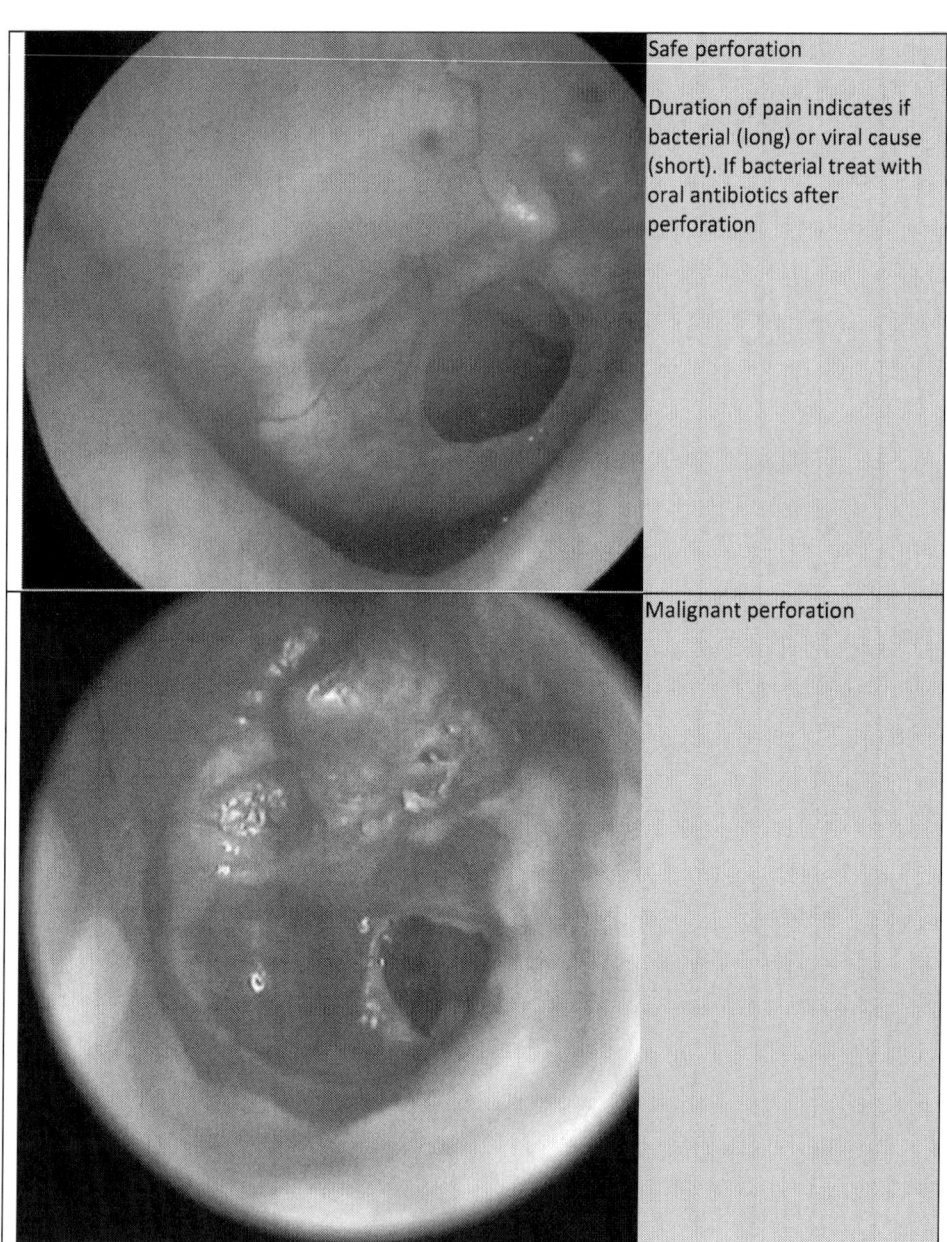

	Safe perforation
	Duration of pain indicates if bacterial (long) or viral cause (short). If bacterial treat with oral antibiotics after perforation
	Malignant perforation

117

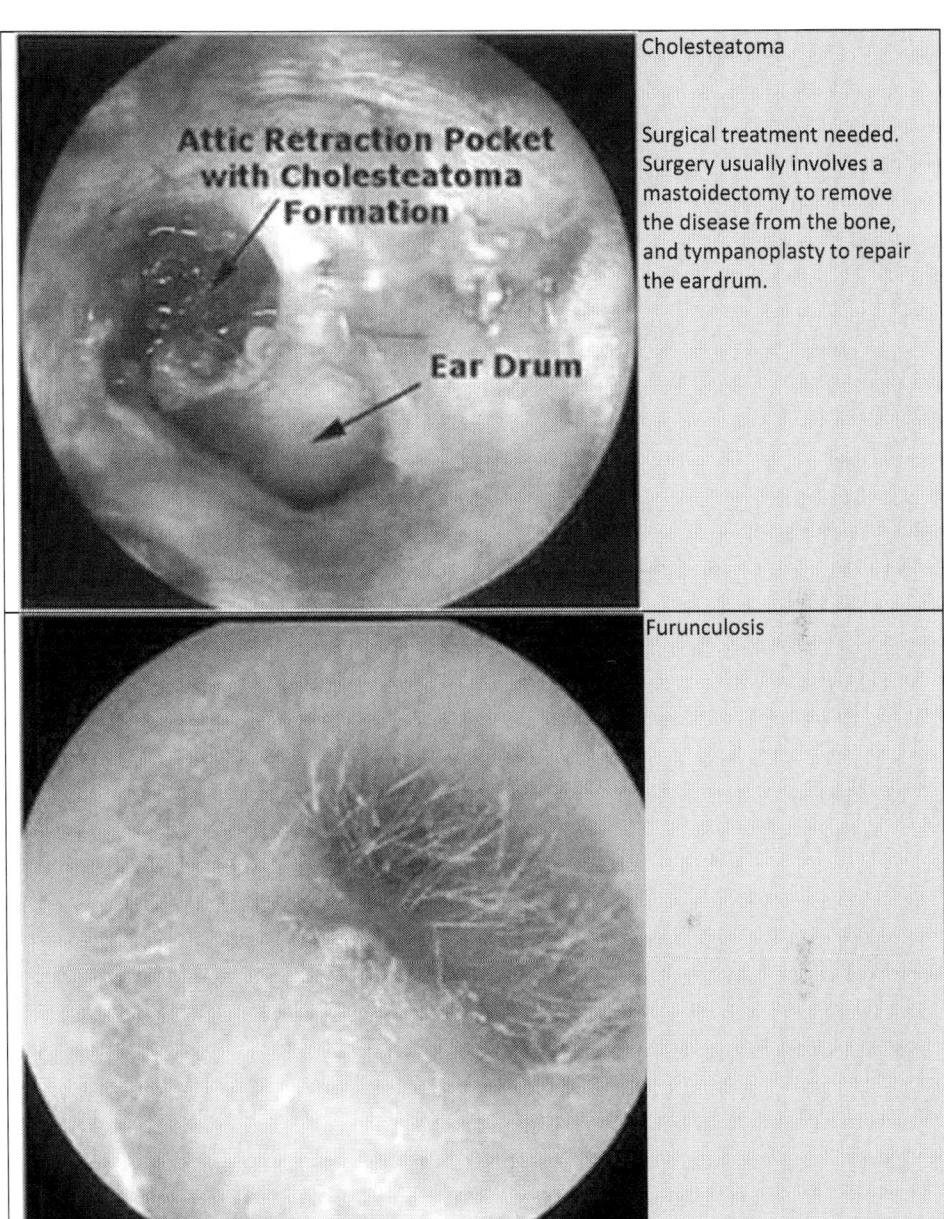

Cholesteatoma

Surgical treatment needed. Surgery usually involves a mastoidectomy to remove the disease from the bone, and tympanoplasty to repair the eardrum.

Furunculosis

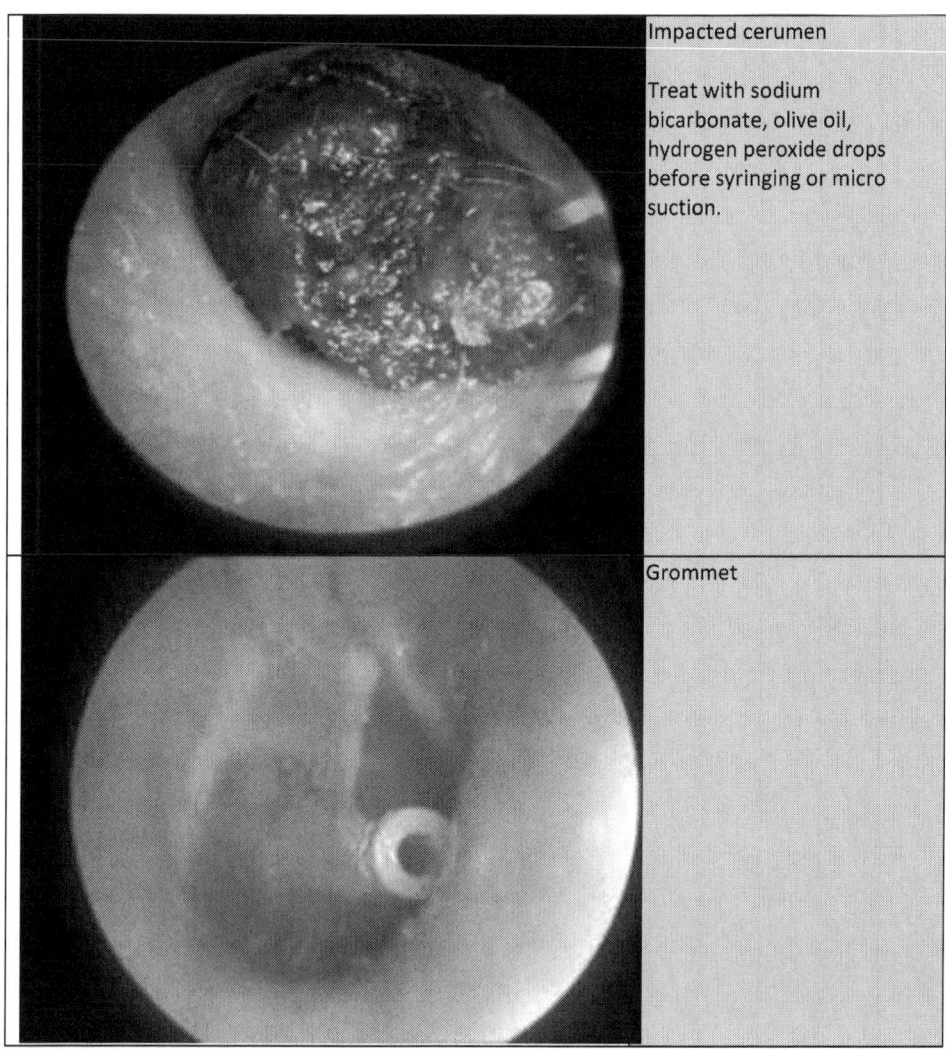

Impacted cerumen
Treat with sodium bicarbonate, olive oil, hydrogen peroxide drops before syringing or micro suction.
Grommet

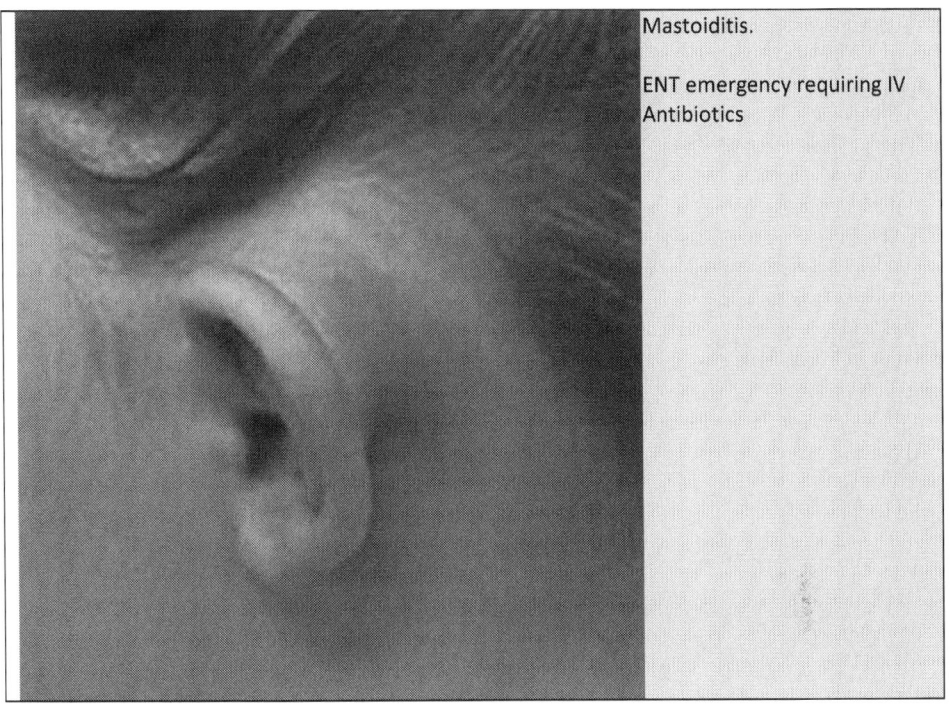

Mastoiditis.

ENT emergency requiring IV Antibiotics

NOSE &
THROAT

Symptoms:

- Blockage (obstruction)
- Runny (rhinorrhoea)
- Pain (focal/general pain)
- Loss of taste or smell (anosmia)
- Itchy eyes

3 types: Allergic, non-allergic and bacterial

Allergic	Non-allergic	Bacterial
Persistent (>4days)	-Pregnancy	<10 days
Asthma is closely linked	-Medicomentosa (rebound effect of overuse of decongestants)	Facial pain
		Anosmia
Investigations:		Mucopurulent discharge
RAST test		>Temperature
Skin prick test		Ear pressure pain
Endoscope		

Management

Topical steroids

Antihistamines.

Antibiotics

Saline irrigation

- Gradual onset
- Lasts more than 12 weeks
- Middle aged patient

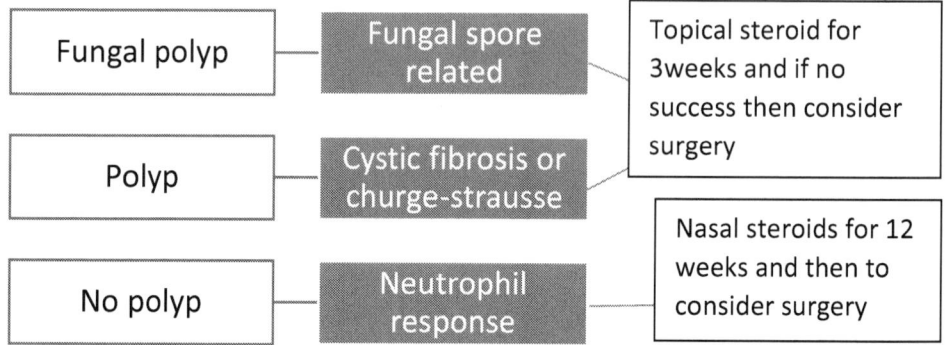

Red flag signs:

-Bleeding, crusting, carcinoma, severe headaches, neurological symptoms.

NOSE BLEEDS

Causes:

- Idiopathic/traumatic
- Anticoagulants
- Leukaemia, Haemophilia
- Haemorrhagic telangiectasia
- Hypertension
- Foreign body
- Neoplasm

Check whether the patient has been coughing up blood which has then entered the nose. Check their past medical history for liver disease.

Management

Pinch nose (10 Minutes)
↓
Intermittent/resolving

Treatment

Naseptin cream (contains peanut)

Beconase spray

Anterior packing with alginate gel

Continued bleeding
↓
visualise area (blow nose)

↓   ↓

Cannot see bleed   Can see bleed

↓   ↓

Anterior packing   Cauterise with

Silver nitrate

Genetic disorder affecting chromosomes 9 and 12. Causes telangectial spotting anywhere on the body, mainly on mucosal surfaces.

Symptoms:

- Nose bleeds
- Rectal bleeds
- Arteriovenous malformation

Affects young men age 15 years old or older. It is a testosterone dependant nasopharyngeal mass. It usually self resolves by 22-25yrs old. A complication is the mass could invade the brain or cause cranial nerve pressure.

Symptoms:

- Nasal blockage(usually unilateral)
- Bleeding large amount

Treatment

Sphenopalatine artery embolism beads

Symptoms:

- Deep ear pain exacerbated by chewing suggests temporomandibular joint dysfunction
- Dental pain should be ruled out by feeling along the gum line
- If there are no sinus symptoms give amitriptyline and conduct a CT scan

STRIDOR

Restricted airflow in the trachea or larynx can cause an inspiratory or biphasic noise.

Symptoms:

- Pyrexia
- Malaise
- Increased respiratory efforts
- Neck swelling
- Tracheal tug
- Intercostal recession
- Positional support

> **Acute treatment**
>
> *Adrenaline* nebuliser (1:1000)
>
> 8mg IV *dexamethasone*
>
> IV antibiotics
>
> Humidified Oxygen

Causes in adults:

- Squamous cell carcinoma
- Bilateral vocal cord palsy
- Thoracic aneurysm
- Thyroid surgery error

Causes of stridor in children:

- Laryngomalacia (very common)

Symptoms of stridor are worse when feeding or crying, they may have a tracheal tug and intercostal recessions.

Some children will outgrow this condition as the walls of the trachea and larynx get stronger. Alternatively, it can be surgically treated by trimming the arytenoid folds

- Glossitis web

Symptoms include a characteristic cry like that of a cat. This condition is surgically corrected.

- Congenital tracheal stenosis

Left pulmonary artery can press onto the trachea causing a stridor. Children tend to outgrow this condition but sometimes it can require extensive surgery.

- Human papilloma virus

Usually affects neonates passing through vaginal canal. Treatment usually involves trimming the swollen vocal cords and it often remits by itself.

THYROGLOSSAL CYST

The most common neck lump. Children aged 5yrs old are mainly affected. It is an embryological remnant of the process where the thyroid moves down from the back of the tongue but in this case does not detach as it would normally. Therefore it will move when swallowing.

Overdose and Electrolyte management

History may be unreliable but aim to identify:

- → What
- → When
- → How much
- → Why
- → With what
- → Pregnant
- → Drug history
- → Past medical history
- → Collateral history

Examine for:

- Trauma
- Stroke/SAH
- Sepsis
- Meningitis
- Electrolyte
- Liver
- Drug level (Salicylate, paracetamol, carboxyHB)

Paracetamol	Bloods at 4 hours – if level >100ml/L give NAC (Parvolax) - Gives angioedema-like reaction.
Digoxin	Digibind
Beta blockers	Glucagon/Atropine
Benzodiazepines	Flumazenil (not for antiepileptic's)
Opioid	Naloxone
Carbon Monoxide	Oxygen
Iron	Desferroxamine
Organophosphates	Atropine
Antifreeze	Alcohol
Cyanide	Hydroxidicobalt
Tricyclic Antidepressant	NaHCO$_3$ / Glucagon / Intralipids
Aspirin	NaHCO$_3$ Check urine is alkaline

Within 4 hours of ingestion:

<1 hour, give activated charcoal - Measure plasma concentrations at 4 hours post ingestion. If levels are above treatment line on treatment graph, give N-acetylcysteine intravenously

Within 4-8 hours of ingestion:

Measure plasma concentrations at presentation and compare concentrations with treatment graph to determine whether N-acetylcysteine should be given

Within 8-15 hours of ingestion:

Take blood for paracetamol concentrations. Start N-acetylcysteine infusion immediately. Stop treatment if level is below the treatment line on the treatment graph.

Within 15-24 hours of ingestion:

Take blood for paracetamol concentrations. Start N-acetylcysteine infusion immediately. If at 24 hours the patient is asymptomatic, INR, blood, gases and plasma creatinine are normal and plasma paracetamol concentration <10mg/L, then the N-acetylcysteine infusion can be stopped. If any of these are abnormal then continue N-acetylcysteine at 150mg/Kg over 24 hours.

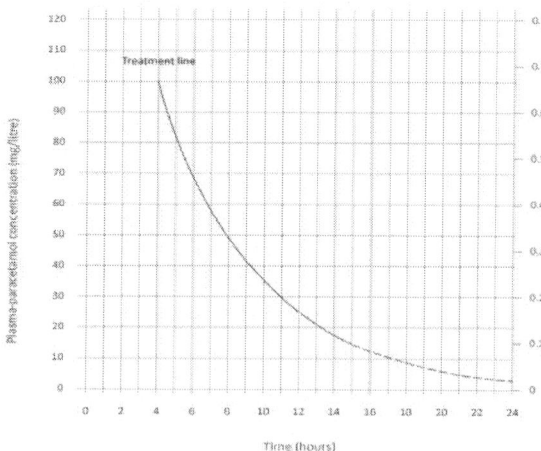

Situations where N-acetylcysteine should be given without guidance of the treatment graph:

- Where timing of overdose is unknown
- Where overdose was staggered (tablets taken at 2 or more times)
- All patients presenting with evidence of severe toxicity

129

Overdose results in hyperventilation and a respiratory alkalosis. This is then followed by a compensatory increase in renal excretion of bicarbonate, sodium, potassium and water, resulting in metabolic acidosis with dehydration and electrolyte imbalance.

If <1hour since overdose and there are no contraindications, perform gastric lavage and give 50g activated charcoal. If >1 hour just give activated charcoal.

Urinary alkalinisation can also be used to enhance the elimination of the drug and reduce its effects on the central nervous system. Give 1 litre of sodium bicarbonate with 40mmol K+ intravenously over 4 hours. Aim for a urine Ph of 7.5 to 8.5.

BENZODIAZEPINES

Provide airway maintenance and ventilatory support if required. Activated charcoal may be given to patients who have taken more than 1mg/kg within 1 hour, providing they are not too drowsy.

The use of flumazenil should not be used as a diagnostic test or in a mixed overdose.

TRICYCLIC ANTIDEPRESSANTS

Patients will present with tachycardia, dry mouth, agitation and dilated pupils. Correct hypoxia with assisted ventilation. Give activated charcoal if it is estimated that the patient has taken more than 5mg/kg within the last hour. A second dose of charcoal should be considered after 2 hours in patients with central features of toxicity. If hypotensive, raise the foot of bed and, if necessary provide intravenous fluids. Monitor ECG until heart rate < 100 bpm, QRS normal and no conduction defect.

Treat arrhythmias by correcting hypoxia and acidosis. Treat seizures with lorazepam, and delirium with oral diazepam. Indications for $NaHCO_3$ are a pH<7.1, QRS>0.6 seconds, or if the patient has developed arrhythmias, hypotension or seizures. The target pH is 7.45-7.55.

<u>Hypo (<Na) (<135)</u>

Symptoms: Nausea and Vomiting, Lethargy, Headaches, Confusion, Seizures, Muscle cramps, Decreased BP.

Investigation: U+E's, urine osmolality, urine sodium concentration

Treatment: increase Na (10-12mmol/L/day) with NORMAL SALINE or water restriction depending on hypervolemia (dilution effect)

Na⁺

<u>Hyper (>Na) (<142)</u>

Symptoms: Nausea, Lethargy, Confusion, Seizures, Coma, Increased BP

Investigation: U+E's, urine osmolality, urine sodium concentration

Treatment: Correct slowly to avoid cerebral oedema with WATER or DEXTROSE 5% IV (if oral is not possible). If hypervolemic stop all Na containing fluids.

Hypo (<K) (<3.5)

Symptoms: None until around <2.5 usually; Nausea and Vomiting, Polyuria, VF, decreased bowel motions, Muscle cramps, paranesthesia.

Investigation: U+E's, ECG; >P-R time, ST depression, prominent U wave.

Treatment: K^+ REPLACEMENT (<20mmol/h), use K sparing diuretics if cause is diuretics. (Amiloride/spironolactone)

K^+

Hyper (>K) (>5)(>6.5 = urgent)

Symptoms: Muscle cramps, Weakness, Abdomen distension, irritability.

Investigation: Serum potassium, ECG; >P-R time, <P wave, broad QRS, >T wave.

Treatment: CALCIUM (GLUCONATE/CHLORIDE) - protects the heart doesn't reverse K^+

INSULIN (over 30mins) + DEXTROSE. Consider stopping ACEi/K+ sparing diuretics.

Hypo (<Ca) (<2.2)

Symptoms: Numb, paresthesia, <BP, Muscular irritability, tetany.

Investigation: Serum calcium, ECG; >QT interval

Treatment: CALCIUM (GLUCONATE/CHLORIDE) (10ml), if chronic give ORAL CALCIUM

Ca^{2+}

Hyper (>Ca) (>2.5)

Symptoms: None/ Bone pain, Confusion, Constipation, Stones, HTN

Investigation: Serum calcium, Serum parathyroid hormone, U+E's, ECG; <ST segment, <QT interval, Bradycardia, heart blocks

Treatment: If malignant cause; SALINE/BISPHOSPHONATES. If Parathyroid: SURGERY. Also consider ORAL STEROIDS

<u>Hypo (<Mg) (<0.7)</u>

Symptoms: Tetany, Seizures, Arrhythmias, Insomnia, Vomiting, Anorexia

Investigation: ECG; Flat/Inverted T wave, >P-R time, wide QRS.

Treatment: oral replacement

Mg⁺

<u>Hyper (>Mg) (>1.1)</u>

Symptoms: Headache, Flushing, Nausea, Arrhythmia

Investigation: Full bloods/electrolytes

Treatment: Stop antacids

The primary survey is a way for any healthcare professional to manage a patient in an acute setting as well lead and organise their care with the relevant multidisciplinary team.

At every point of the Primary Survey you should identify any issues, request investigations and treat them for those issues before moving on to the next stage. It consists of:

Taking a good history, this will help you identify a few differentials. Once you have an idea of the specialty this falls under, state that you would call for help from that specialty doctor. If being examined, explain to the examiner your main concern is ____ but that you would follow the main ABCDE system described below.

Airway

Is the airway patent? You can check for this by seeing if the patient can talk to you or is gasping for breath. Also listen for any stridor or gurgling from airway secretions. If there is airway blockage you may need to use suction. Remember to jaw-thrust unless c-spine injury if needed for:

- Nasopharyngeal airway (do not use in basal skull fracture)
- Oropharyngeal airway (insert upside down and twist in)
- Laryngeal mask airways (iGels)

Breathing

How are their oxygen saturations? Attach a sats probe and assess their respiration rate. You also want to check their chest is equally expanding and listen to the chest for equal air entry. Feel for a central trachea. Any patient in an acute setting should be given a **15L rebreather oxygen mask**. If you do not hear equal air entry on the chest you should percuss the chest to see if there is signs of pneumothorax. If there is, then begin thoracocentesis.

Investigations that can be requested – X-Ray, ABG, sputum culture

Treatments – Nebulisers (side effect is high heart rate), IM adrenaline (side effect is high blood pressure), 24-28% oxygen (type 2 respiratory failure patients e.g. COPD), anti-histamines IM.

Circulation

Are they haemodynamically stable? Check their appearance for raised JVP, pallor, cyanosis, also check their pulse and capillary refill. At this point you need to monitor their **blood pressure, urine output** and gain venous access with a **cannula** in case they require fluids and to request blood tests. Finally, auscultate the heart.

Investigations that can be requested – ECG, Echo, bloods: FBC, U&E, LFTs, Crossmatch, Culture + any specific blood test necessary to the patients suspected diagnosis (mast cell tryptan, troponin, uric acid, amylase, platelets)

Treatments – IV fluids (500ml saline), IV blood, IV antibiotics, IV steroids (100-200ml), Diuretics

Disability

Are they confused or unconscious? Check the patient's level of awareness with **AVPU** or GCS scoring. Also check their blood **glucose** in case that is the cause of unconsciousness. Also check their body temperature. Focal tests for meningitis (paediatric patients)

Investigations that can be requested – BM, Babinski test

Treatment – 50ml 50% glucose / 100ml 20% glucose

Exposure

Are there any other signs? Expose the patient to check for scars, blood, and trauma and also assess limb tone.

<u>Signs of deterioration</u>

Always remember that the order of distress signs will go:

Respiratory rate	
Heart rate	if all three are deranged then the patient is in
Blood pressure	'shock'

<u>The reversible causes are remembered by the "4 Hs and 4 Ts"</u>

O   Hypoxia: ensure a patent airway and give high flow oxygen

O   Hypovolaemia: commence IV fluid resuscitation (Leads to PEA) (Can be anaphylaxis)

O   Hypo/hyperkalaemia and other metabolic derangements: check the VBG for any metabolic derangements and correct accordingly

O   Hypothermia (Can lead to bradycardia to VF)

O   Tension pneumothorax (Can cause PEA) treat with thoracocentesis

O   Tamponade (cardiac): obtain a beside echocardiogram (echo) and perform pericardiocentesis as indicated

O   Toxins: check the patient's drug chart and/or enquire about recent medications or overdoses in the collateral history (opioid, cyanide, and digoxin)

O   Thrombosis (pulmonary or cardiac) (Can cause PEA)

In paediatric cases:

Ensure you ask the patient if they're the mother, why partner could not be present, if any injuries have happened before and if there is any previous admissions to hospital. Also ask if they think the partner could have injured the child.

To assess hydration status evaluate the fontanelle, how many wet nappies there have been and blood pressure.

Be sure to test for focal signs of meningitis by tilting the chin down to see if the knees flex inwards. In cases of suspected meningitis always request a lumbar puncture and start antibiotics.

In suspected fractures always assess neurovascular status before calling orthopaedics.

Respiratory rate and Heart rate are unreliable factors if the child is in pain or crying.

137

Solo responder role:

Check it's safe to approach

Shake to wake

Check carotid and breath sounds

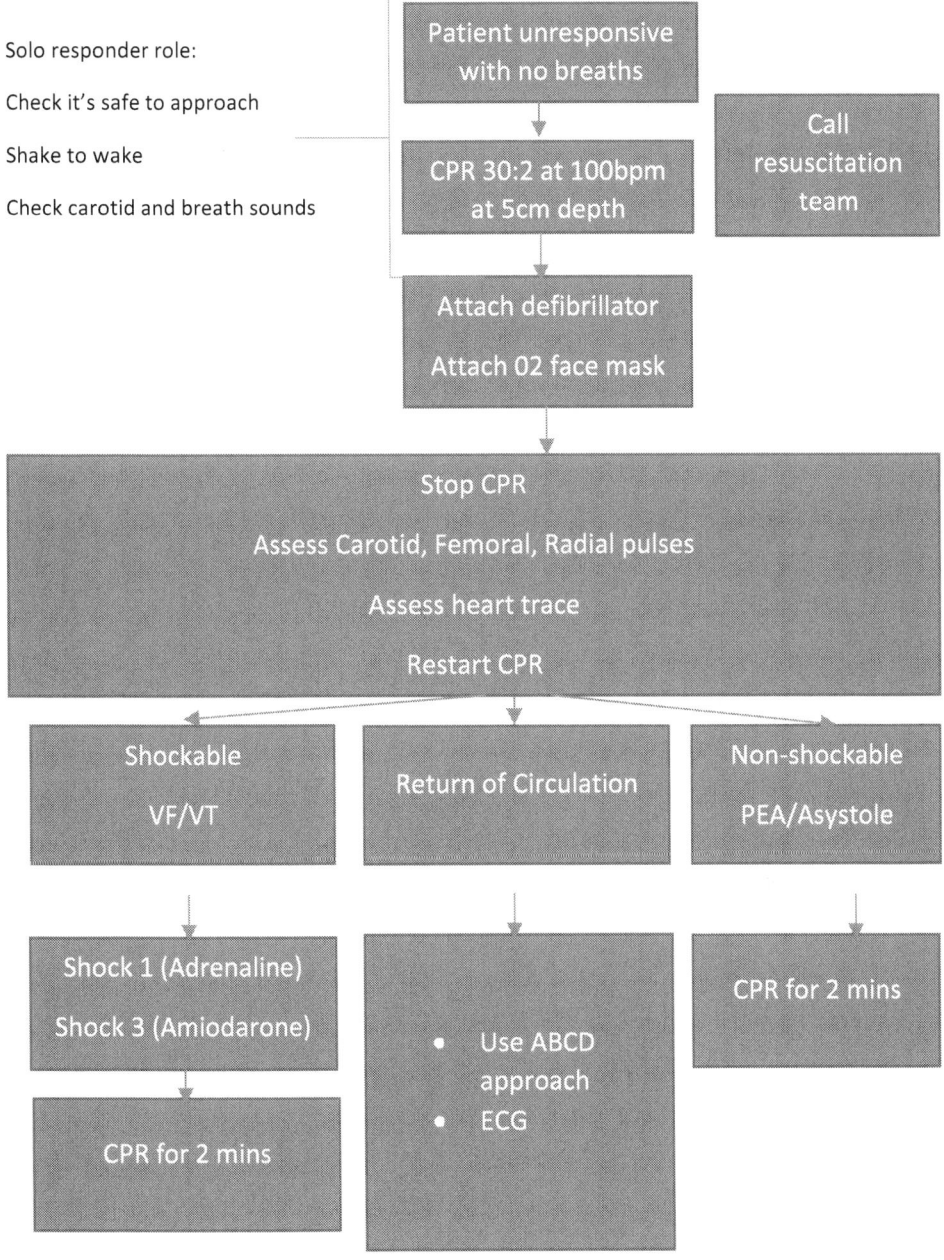

Patient unresponsive with no breaths

Call resuscitation team

CPR 30:2 at 100bpm at 5cm depth

Attach defibrillator

Attach 02 face mask

Stop CPR

Assess Carotid, Femoral, Radial pulses

Assess heart trace

Restart CPR

Shockable

VF/VT

Return of Circulation

Non-shockable

PEA/Asystole

Shock 1 (Adrenaline)

Shock 3 (Amiodarone)

CPR for 2 mins

- Use ABCD approach
- ECG

CPR for 2 mins

Orthopaedics

Decreased bone mineral density compared to the average younger adult. Bone mineral density testing should be recommended to all postmenopausal women who are 65 years of age or older with a DEXA scan.

Treatment

Calcium (*Adcal*) / bisphosphonates (*Alendronic acid*) (require 30mins standing or sitting when taking to prevent reflux).

Primary: Overuse and old age
Secondary: Avascular necrosis, Trauma, Developmental, Misalignment post Op

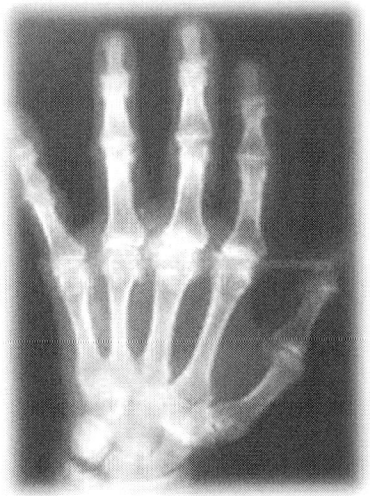

4 key signs on X-Ray

- No space between the joins
- Sclerosis at the joint surface (very white)
- Osteophytes (bone spurs)
- Subchondral Cysts (pockets of synovium)

Treatment

Rest / Aids / Injections / Bracing / Arthroplasty / Arthrodesis

- ○ Patient details and X-ray view (AP/PA)
- ○ Rotation (space between the clavicles and if spinous processes run linearly)
- ○ Exposure (can you see the entirety of the lung edges)
- ○ Inspiration (can you see 5 ribs anteriorly and 7 ribs posteriorly)
- ○ Trachea (check if deviated or not)
- ○ Cardiomegaly (cardio thoracic ratio)
- ○ Upper lobe diversions (more blood vessels in upper lobes – the normal vascular markings would show greater blood supply in the lower lobes)
- ○ Blunting of costophrenic angles
- ○ Any opacity in the lungs

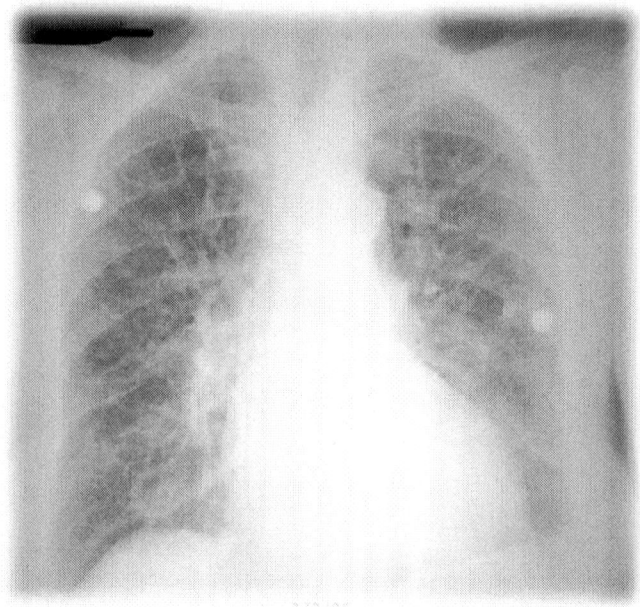

Rib fracture/injury

Pain gets worse a few days after trauma, maximum pain at 48 hours. These can often resolve on their own.

Falls

How did you land?	When did chest start hurting?	
Where was the pain first?	Has pain gotten worse?	Any cough?
Did you get yourself up?	What makes it hurt?	Fever?

On examination check for surgical emphysema (pneumothorax), trachea central, feel for chest flail. Listen to chest and hold chest fixed to listen/feel for pop/click. Check for splenic rupture.

Dislocations

Shoulder: Always check deltoid sensation, anterior dislocation is more common. Posterior dislocations only occurs from electrocution or seizures.

Ankle: Actually fractures most of the time, therefore reduce the fracture immediately

ABDOMINAL X-RAYS

On X-ray you should not be able to view the small bowel. The large bowel however should have some air inside and show the haustral folds.

The small bowel would only show up in an obstruction of the small bowel. The usual haustrae of the small bowel would present as plicae circulares across the width of the small bowel. Also no air will be present in the large bowel indicating there is an obstruction proximal to it.

If the large bowel presents with no haustrae but is very distended with air, this indicates a blockage distal to the large bowel e.g. stricture, cancer, foreign body in rectum.

With any obstruction it is important to request an erect x-ray to check for any air under the diaphragm which would signify rupture. A CT could also be requested to see the level of the obstruction but renal function needs to be assessed before a CT can take place.

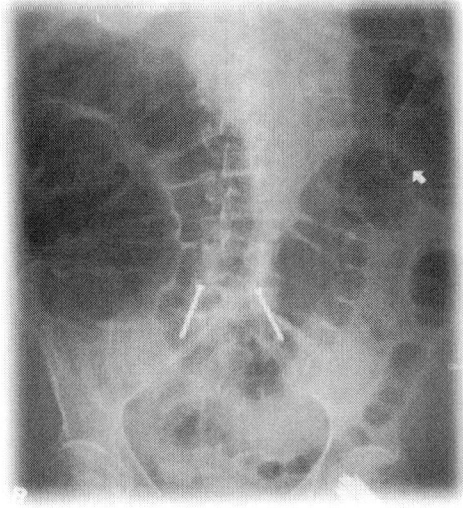

$\frac{1}{3}$ Recover to similar mobility. 4:1 female to male. 30% mortality. Poor quality of life.

Blood supply = Obturator artery (10%), lateral and medial femoral circumflex artery.

Capsular margins = Greater trochanter + Lesser trochanter + acetabulum

Treatment

Take History, AMTS, and kidney function.

Operate within 36 hours. Immediate O_2, fluids and opioid (check kidneys can handle it) or fascia illiaca block (anaesthetise upper $\frac{1}{3}$ along from ASIS to Pubic symphysis) (lateral femoral cutaneous nerve).

Extracapsular fracture = Bone can be fixed together and will heal as blood supply remains. Dynamic hip screws/ intramedullary nail + pins.

Intracapsular fractures = Subcapital/transcervical/basicervical all require hip replacement (disrupts bloods supply to femoral head risking avascular necrosis). Hemiarthroplasty / Total hip replacement.

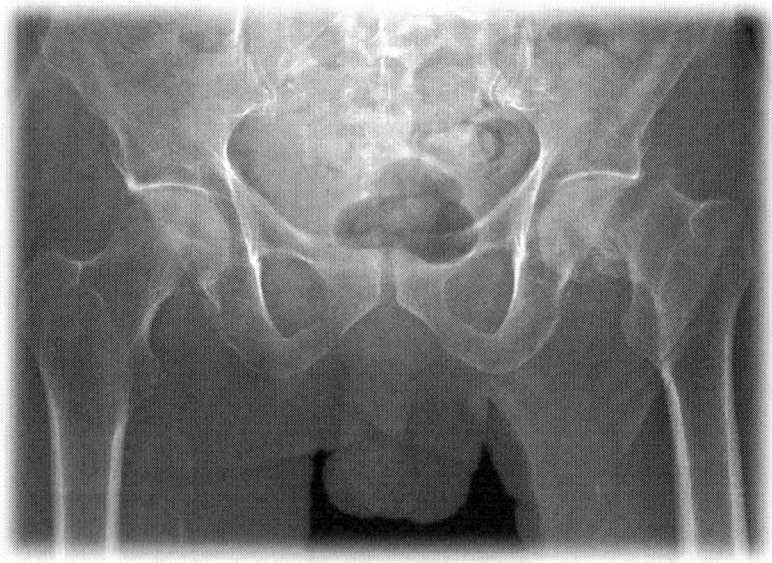

Fractures of the femoral neck present with a shortened and externally rotated leg whereas femoral head fractures present with a shortened but internally rotated leg.

Head of femur should not be below the line of lesser trochanter and neck of femur. It should be partly raised above it. If lower this suggests a slipped epiphysis. There are 5 types:

S=slipped(1) A=above epiphysis(2) L=lower than epiphysis(3) T=through epiphysis(4)
R=rammed (compressed epiphysis)(5)

FRACTURE X-RAYS

Whenever describing X-Ray fractures always:

- Patient details and X-ray view (anterior + lateral) and say which bone is the focus
- Follow the outer borders of the bones to find any breaks. Compare the suspected bone with the normal counter bone in the opposite limb (if only bones are injured on one side of the body)
- Describe the type of fracture + extra/intracapsular, describing the distal part not the proximal
- Describe the extent of the fracture (e.g. subtrochlear fracture)
- Beware of growth plates which have yet to fuse in children, these are not fractures!
- Mention LARA :

Length (has the bone shortened or is there now a fracture space) Usually easy to tell because the upper boarders of the affected bone will not be in the anatomically correct place or not in line with where they should be (e.g. the ulnar styloid should be lower than the radial styloid)
Apposition (along transverse plane) (describe which bone it is translated towards e.g. radially translated)
Rotation (the non-fractured part of the bone will look different to its counterpart because it is rotated)
Angulation (Dorsally/Palmar (volar))

Types of fracture: transverse, oblique (opposing muscle contractions), spiral (in young children always query abuse), stress (e.g. from long marching).

Follow the same rules of describing fracture X-rays.

Some fractures only occur in children: Green stick and Torus fractures

These can also be intra or extracapsular. As the radius and ulnar are closely tied together there can be damage to one bone and the fibres between or damage to both bones. Remember the normal anatomical lines when looking for fractures here and when looking to see if anything is shortened or lengthened. (Ulnar styloid should not be higher than the radial styloid)

Anterior fractures: Smith's   Posterior fractures: Colle's

Check neurological function of these patients with:

Median nerve motor supply = Fingers 1, 2, 3.   Test = 'Ok' sign

Ulnar nerve motor supply = Finger 4.   Test = 'Fingers crossed' sign

Radial nerve motor supply = Thumb   Test = 'Thumbs up' sign

Treatment

Haematoma block (anaesthetic into haematoma), manipulation; tug the fingers and move in the opposite direction of deformity. Clean and splint. Surgical treatment: K-wires/ metal plate.

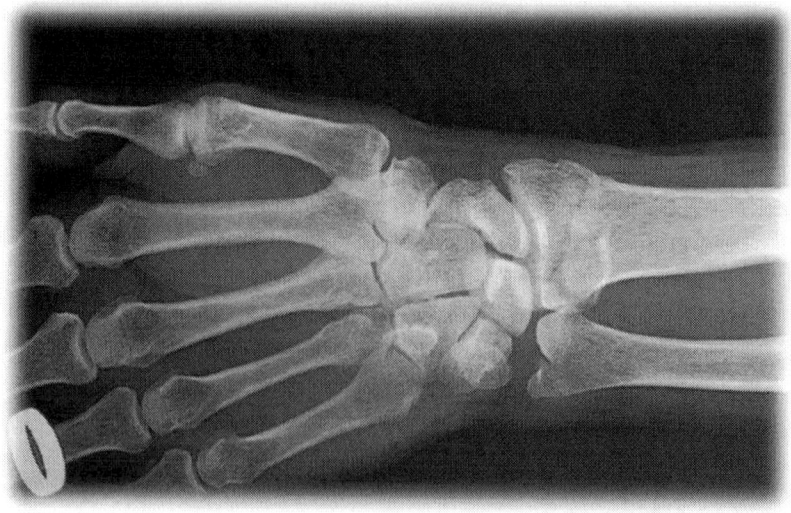

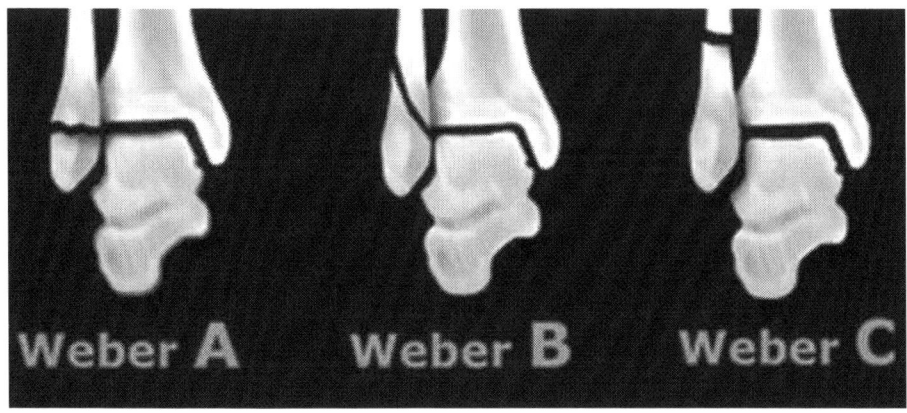

The joint between the tibia and fibula (the inferior tibiofibular ligament) is called 'syndesmoses.

Fractures below this level are called a <u>Weber A</u> (Can be placed in plaster/boot and heal)

Fractures at this level are called a <u>Weber B</u> (Can displace Talus causing sore ankle - Surgery)

Fractures above this level are called a <u>Weber C</u> (force has gone through the ligament, therefore the joint is very loose. Early arthritis can occur if not treated)

<u>Tendonitis</u>

Do a squeeze test to identify if there is rupture of the Achilles tendon.

COMPARTMENT SYNDROME

Both arm and leg fractures can cause bleeding into the tissue compartments and compress the Vein, Artery and Nerve (VAN) running through. This can occur in open or closed fractures. Most commonly it will present in the lower legs but can take place in the upper limbs too. Pressure should not be more than a 30mmHg difference between blood pressure and compartment pressure.

Missed compartment syndrome (>6 hours):

- Cold
- Pulseless
- Loss of sensation
- Increased capillary refill time

Onset of compartment syndrome (<6 hours):

- Swollen
- Painful (disproportional pain compared to injury, doesn't ease with analgesia, hurts if finger or toe are flexed)
- Very tense

Treatment: Fasciotomy

SEPTIC ARTHRITIS

Irreversible damage after 8 hours

Symptoms:

- Holding the join in the position of maximal fluid (e.g. Hip flexed, externally rotated and abducted)
- Cannot move the joint
- Fever

Check patient's bloods (ESR, CRP, WCC), aspirate the joint and give antibiotics.

Treatment

Arthroscopy debridement.

Children who cannot walk

The most likely the cause for immobility is because the hip is septic or has structural damage.

Structural hip pathology can be e.g. fluid effusion, Perthe's disease (6-8yrs old) or a slipped epiphyseal plate. Rule out sepsis by checking bloods (CRP, ESR, WCC), fever and X-ray.

PLASTER REMOVAL

	Child	Adult
Upper Limb	3 week	6 week
Lower Limb	6 week	12 week

Causes include duodenal perforation, genitourinary perforation, small bowel perforation, laproscopy and ERCP perforation. The air trapped in the peritoneum causes acute peritonitis.

Symptoms:

- Pain (worse when coughing)
- Fever
- Vomiting
- Guarding (relaxing the muscle causes pain)
- Low blood pressure
- High heart rate

Investigations: Amylase, FBC, LFT, U+E, Catheter, Erect chest X-Ray.

Treatment: long term PPI, Antibiotics, Nil by mouth, Fluids.

Dermatology

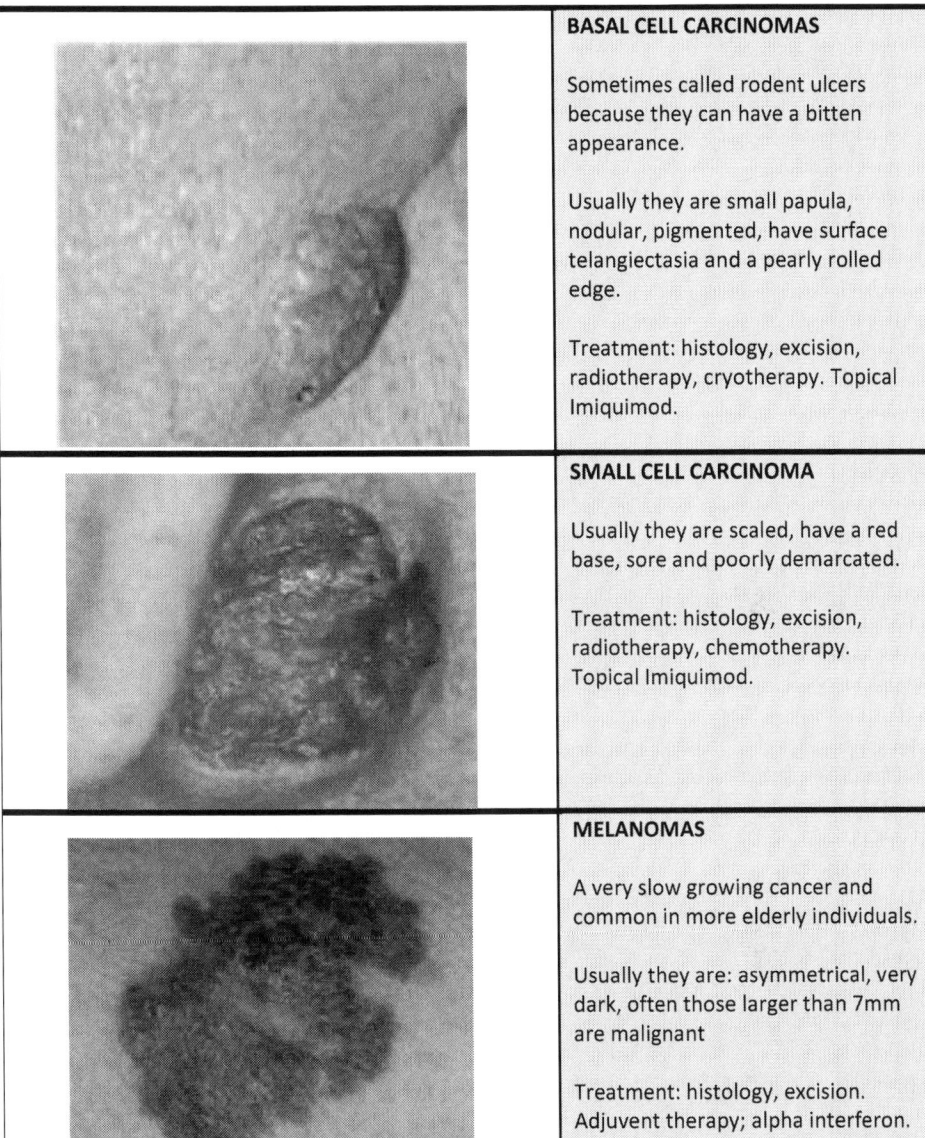

BASAL CELL CARCINOMAS

Sometimes called rodent ulcers because they can have a bitten appearance.

Usually they are small papula, nodular, pigmented, have surface telangiectasia and a pearly rolled edge.

Treatment: histology, excision, radiotherapy, cryotherapy. Topical Imiquimod.

SMALL CELL CARCINOMA

Usually they are scaled, have a red base, sore and poorly demarcated.

Treatment: histology, excision, radiotherapy, chemotherapy. Topical Imiquimod.

MELANOMAS

A very slow growing cancer and common in more elderly individuals.

Usually they are: asymmetrical, very dark, often those larger than 7mm are malignant

Treatment: histology, excision. Adjuvent therapy; alpha interferon.

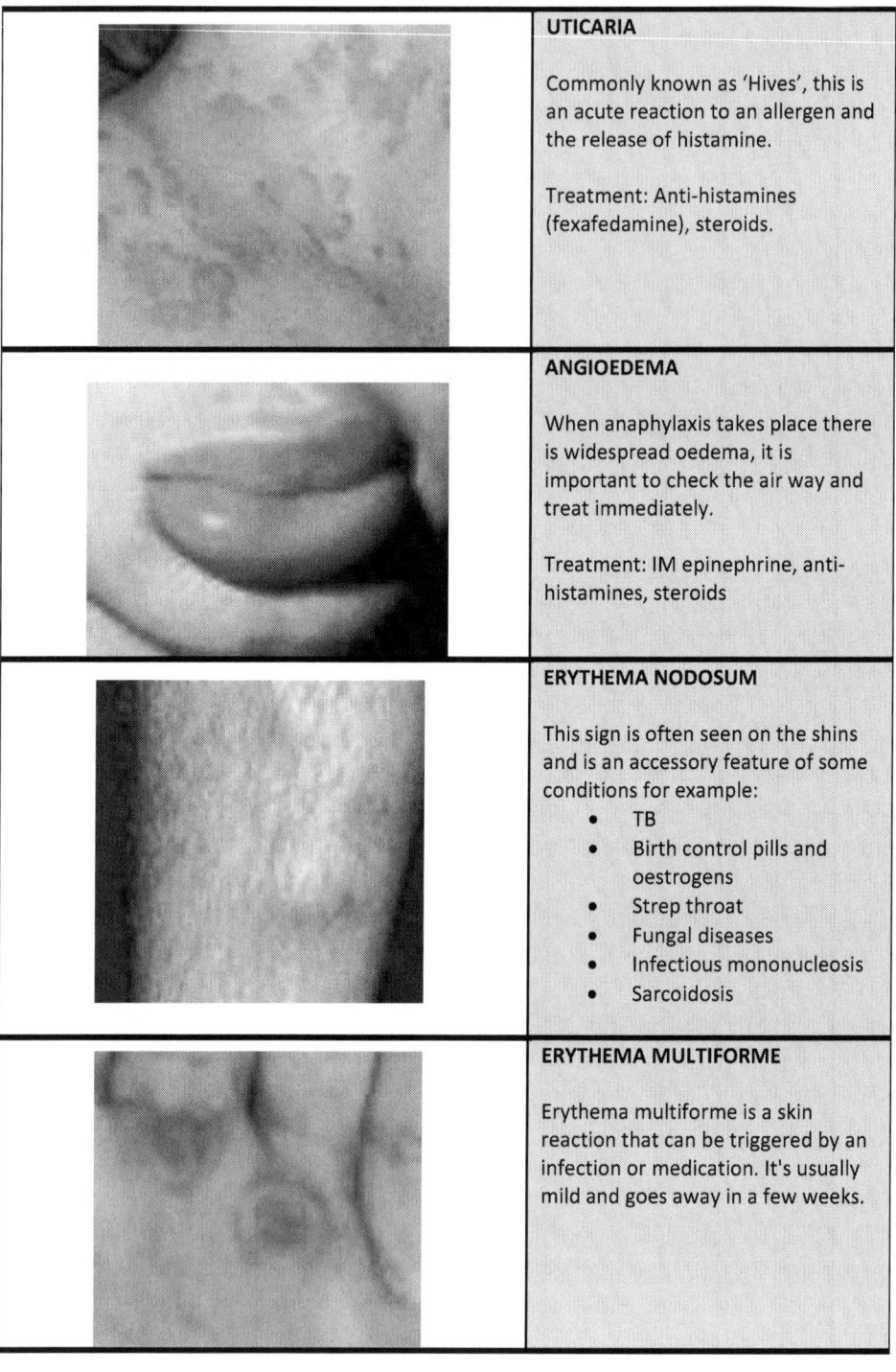

	UTICARIA
	Commonly known as 'Hives', this is an acute reaction to an allergen and the release of histamine.
	Treatment: Anti-histamines (fexafedamine), steroids.
	ANGIOEDEMA
	When anaphylaxis takes place there is widespread oedema, it is important to check the air way and treat immediately.
	Treatment: IM epinephrine, anti-histamines, steroids
	ERYTHEMA NODOSUM
	This sign is often seen on the shins and is an accessory feature of some conditions for example: <ul><li>TB</li><li>Birth control pills and oestrogens</li><li>Strep throat</li><li>Fungal diseases</li><li>Infectious mononucleosis</li><li>Sarcoidosis</li></ul>
	ERYTHEMA MULTIFORME
	Erythema multiforme is a skin reaction that can be triggered by an infection or medication. It's usually mild and goes away in a few weeks.

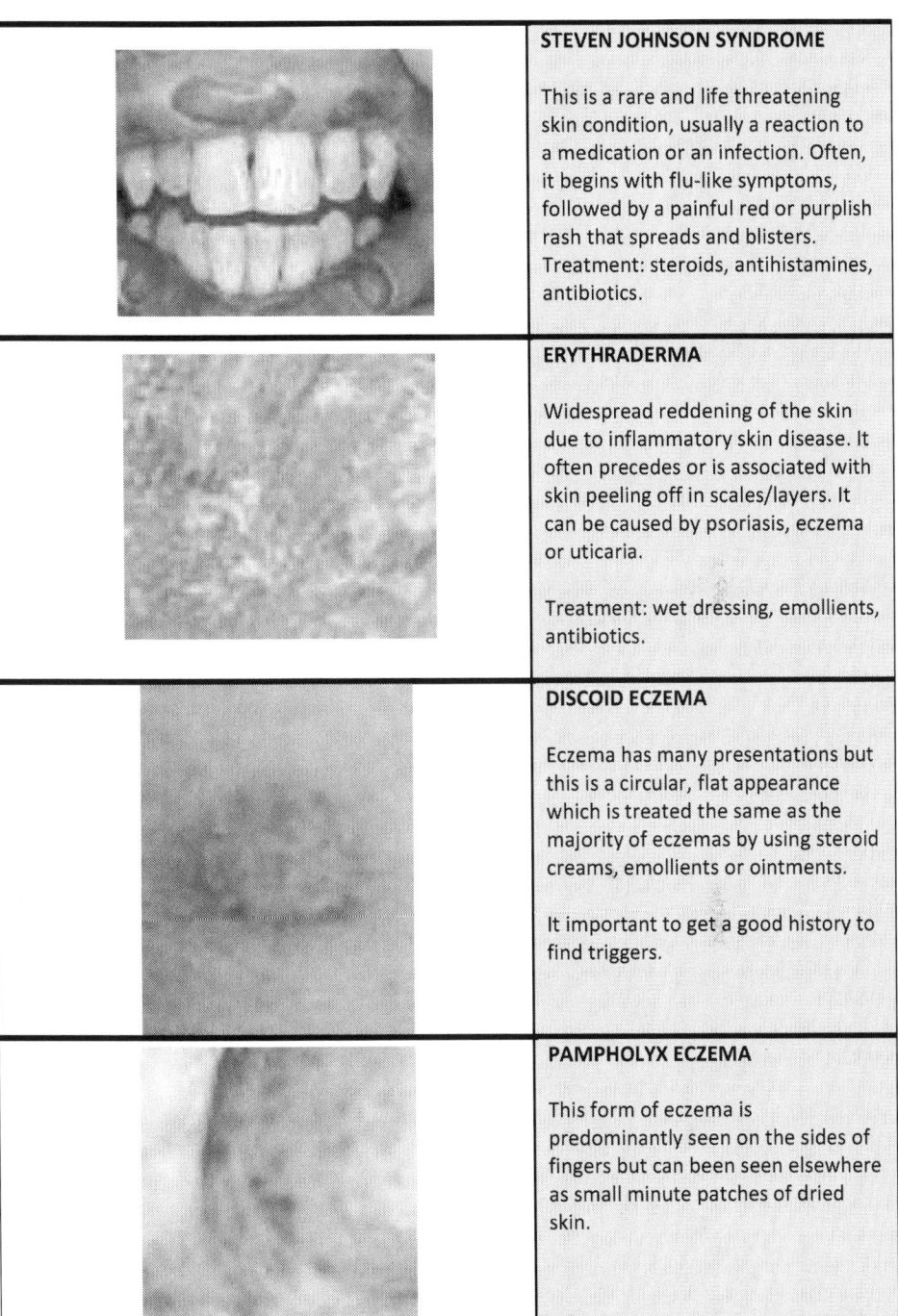

	STEVEN JOHNSON SYNDROME This is a rare and life threatening skin condition, usually a reaction to a medication or an infection. Often, it begins with flu-like symptoms, followed by a painful red or purplish rash that spreads and blisters. Treatment: steroids, antihistamines, antibiotics.
	ERYTHRADERMA Widespread reddening of the skin due to inflammatory skin disease. It often precedes or is associated with skin peeling off in scales/layers. It can be caused by psoriasis, eczema or uticaria. Treatment: wet dressing, emollients, antibiotics.
	DISCOID ECZEMA Eczema has many presentations but this is a circular, flat appearance which is treated the same as the majority of eczemas by using steroid creams, emollients or ointments. It important to get a good history to find triggers.
	PAMPHOLYX ECZEMA This form of eczema is predominantly seen on the sides of fingers but can been seen elsewhere as small minute patches of dried skin.

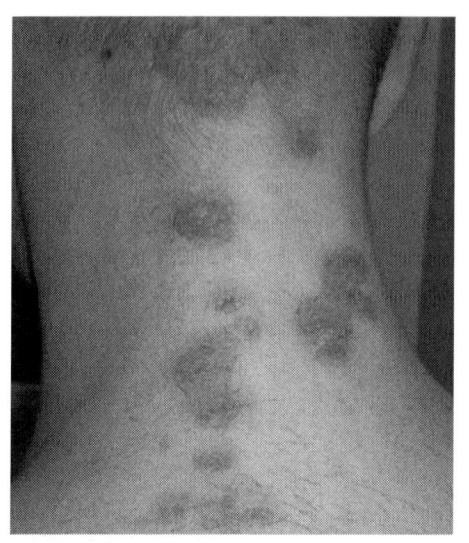

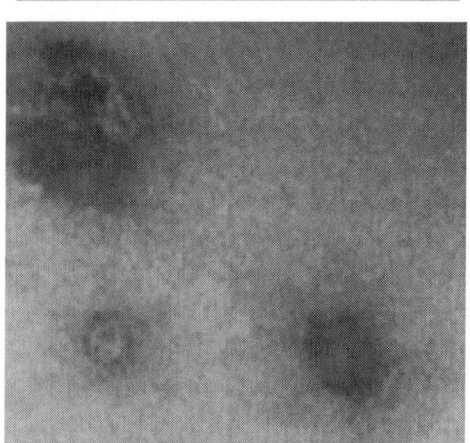

IMPETIGO

The infection shown here typically occurs via skin breakage from excoriation or skin diseases. It is first characterized by a red macule or papule that turns into a fragile vesicle. The vesicle then develops into a superficial flaccid bulla, with surrounding erythema and later ruptures to become a yellow–crusted papule or plaque. The lesions are typically asymptomatic, with occasional pain or pruritus.

Impetigo is a gram-positive bacterial infection of the superficial layers of the epidermis; the most common causative organisms are *S aureus* and *Strep pyogenes*. Symptoms include pruritic blisters, lymphadenopathy, and skin sores.

Treatment for impetigo is typically with topical antibiotics (e.g., mupirocin, retapamulin) and local wound care.

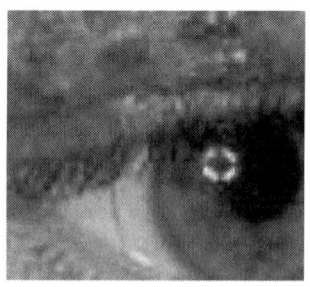

ECZEMA HERPETICUM

This eczema is infected with a herpes virus, it is important to rapidly treat this to avoid the patient going blind if located near the orbit.

Treatment: IV Acyclovir

	PITYRIASIS VERSICOLOR Often associated with excessive sweating, this condition is named for its pale appearance in darker skin and dark appearance on pale skin. Treatment: antifungal shampoo
	VITILIGO Absence of pigment, can be associated with Diabetes type 2 or is congenital.
	XANTHOMATA High cholesterol or lipids in the blood can present with small raised collections under the skin. Treatment: excision, laser, chemical
	PSORIASIS Rapidly cycling of skin maturation causes shedding of skin. Treatment: Emollient, steroid, vit D analogue, coal tar, UV light.

	PLAQUE PSORIASIS A form of psoriasis (one of the 5), that presents with raised plaques, usually on extensor surfaces. Treatment is the same as psoriasis.
	LICHINIFICATION The scratching of skin causes the skin to thicken, hence the term 'lichen' which means thickening.
	KELOID SCAR Over growth of skin. Treatment includes: 1. Freezing early keloids with liquid nitrogen to stop them growing. 2. Laser treatment to reduce redness 3. Surgery, sometimes followed by radiotherapy.
	ACNE Treatment includes: • Stop smoking • Wash 2-3 times a day, avoid oil moisturisers/cosmetics • Salicylic acid(topical) • Clindamycin(topical)/ • Lymecycline (teratogenic) • Isotretinoin (topical retinoid)

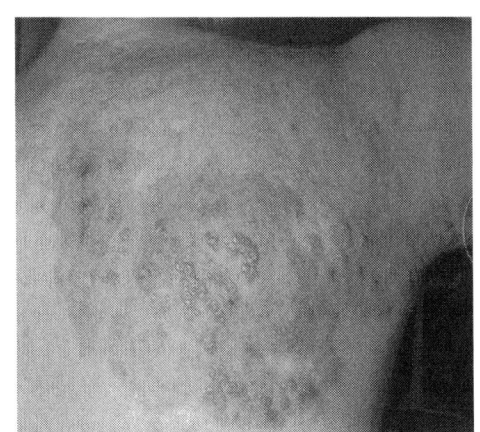

SHINGLES – HSV

Immunodeficiency/immunosuppression, medications or stress are possible triggers. It is a reactivation of the chickenpox virus.

Erythema, regional lymphadenopathy, and grouped vesicles develop, with findings typically being unilateral and usually not crossing the midline (as they travel along the nerve supplying the dermatome)

Treatment for neural pain is amitriptyline

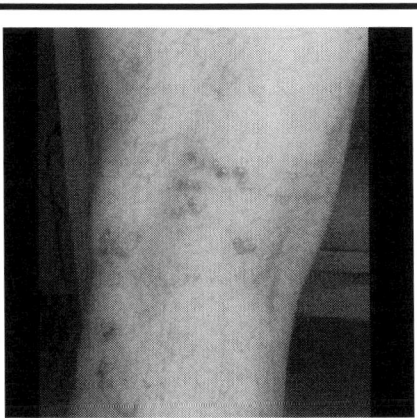

HERPES ZOSTER

Clusters of vesicles are initially clear but they may then become cloudy and may rupture, or crust. For some individuals, the pain does not resolve and may persist for years (neuralgia).

Antiviral agents given early in the disease course may shorten the recovery period and decrease the chance of post herpetic neuralgia.

HSV 1 & 2

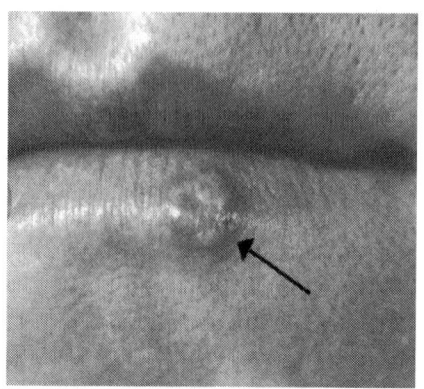

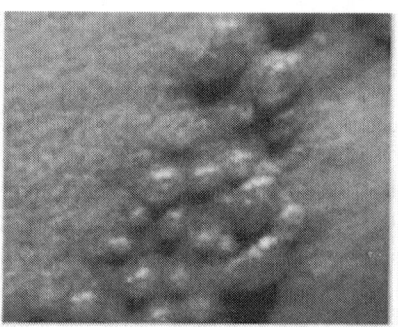

Viruses that cause acute skin infections as grouped vesicles on an erythematous base. HSV-1 usually occurs around the mouth or face while HSV-2 usually occurs on the genitals, buttocks, or anal area.

Infection results from transmission of body fluids onto a mucous membrane or open skin to a susceptible person.

Although there is no cure, most infections are self-limited, and antiviral therapy (e.g. acyclovir) will shorten the course of symptoms and may help to prevent transmission.

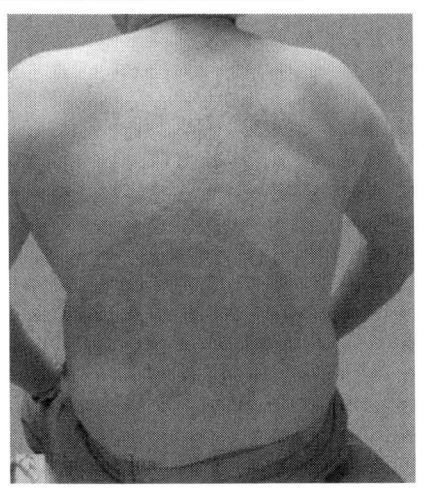

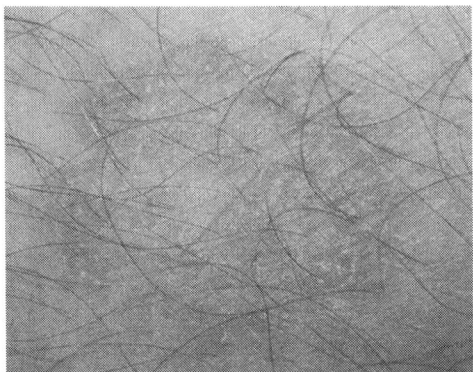

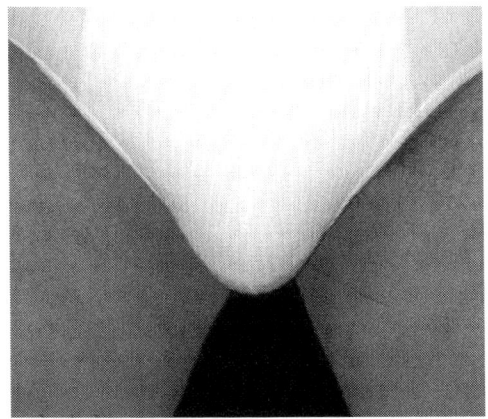

TINEA

Transmission is via direct skin-to-skin contact. Patients may be asymptomatic or complain of a prurititis. The lesion appears as an erythematous, scaly plaque that may enlarge rapidly.

Tinea is a superficial infection characterized by scaly, patches. Its classification is based on the affected region, such as tinea pedis for feet ("athlete's foot"), tinea corporis for body, tinea capitis for head/scalp, and tinea cruris for groin.

They preferentially inhabit warm, moist areas of the skin. Diagnosis may be made with a potassium hydroxide (KOH) preparation from a skin scraping.

Treatment options for tinea include topical antifungal therapy. Some cases may require antibiotics to treat secondary bacterial skin infections that result from scratching.

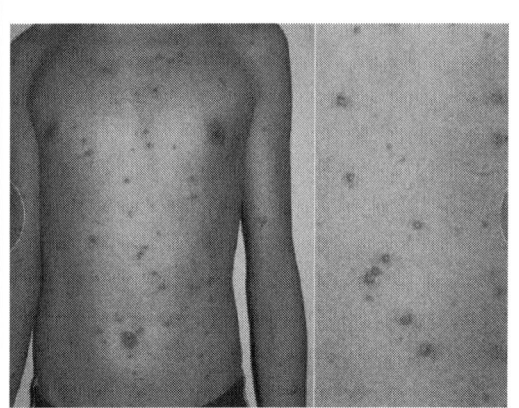

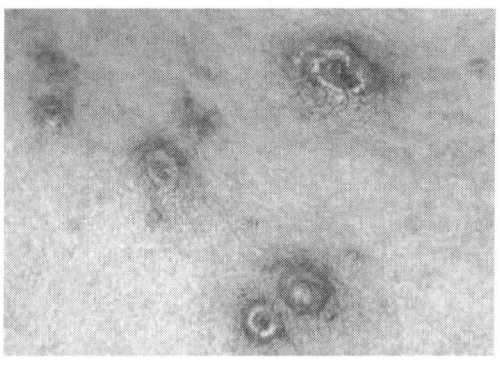

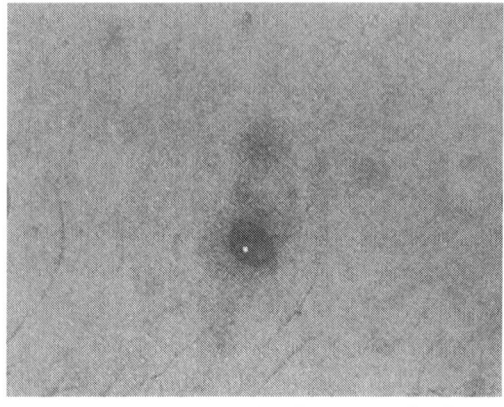

CHICKENPOX

Chickenpox, caused by varicella-zoster virus (VZV), which is highly contagious and acquired via inhalation of airborne respiratory droplets or direct vesicle contact.

This occurs mostly in children younger than 10 years, generally appearing 10-21 days after contact with an infected person. It presents first on the face, torso, or scalp, followed by the rest of the body.

The clear vesicles become central lesions and finally crust. The disease usually resolves spontaneously over 5-10 days. Treatment is generally supportive. However, adults may have significant morbidity from systemic involvement and are often given antiviral medications as early as possible.

Avoid aspirin (associated with Reyes syndrome) and ibuprofen (associated with severe secondary infections).

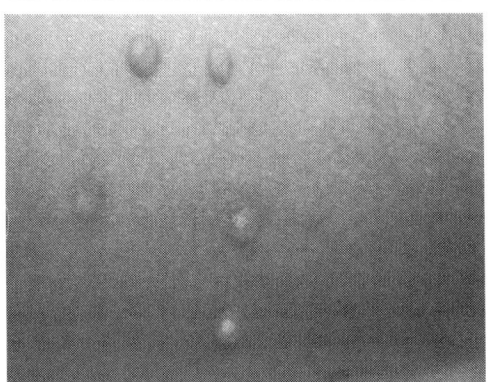

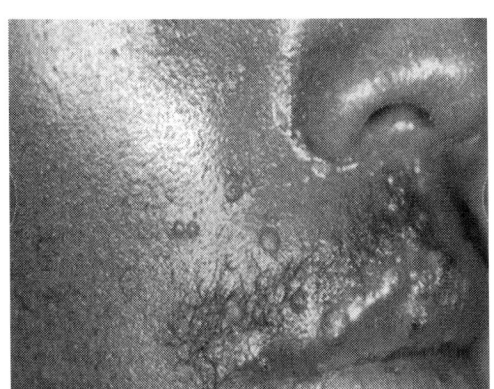

MOLLUSCUM CONTAGIOSUM

Lesions that appeared as firm, smooth, umbilicated papules.

Molluscum contagiosum manifests as raised, pearl-like papules/nodules with a central depression and a plug of cheesy material

Affected areas include the face, neck, armpits, arms, and hands (from direct skin contact or sharing of contaminated towels, sports equipment, or toys), as well as the genitals (from sexual contact).

Topical therapeutic agents may include cantharidin, tretinoin cream, salicylic acid, iodine, and KOH

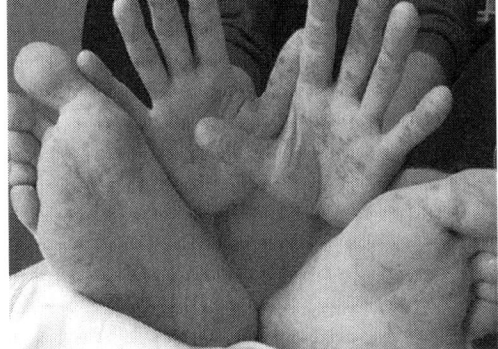

HAND-FOOT-AND-MOUTH

Cutaneous lesions on the hands, feet, and buttocks. Commonly caused by coxsackie virus and typically affects children and infants.

It is highly contagious during the first week of infection and may spread from direct contact with infected material. The incubation period is 3-7 days.

Symptoms include fever, rash, headache, sore throat, oropharyngeal ulcers, and loss of appetite. The oral lesions are normally small vesicles on an erythematous base.

Care is typically supportive.

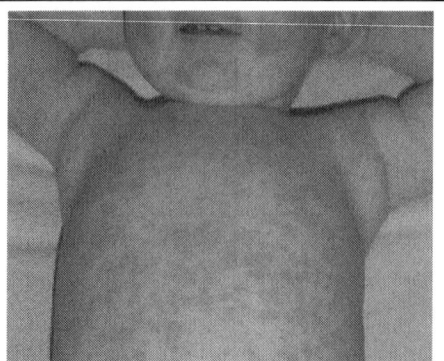

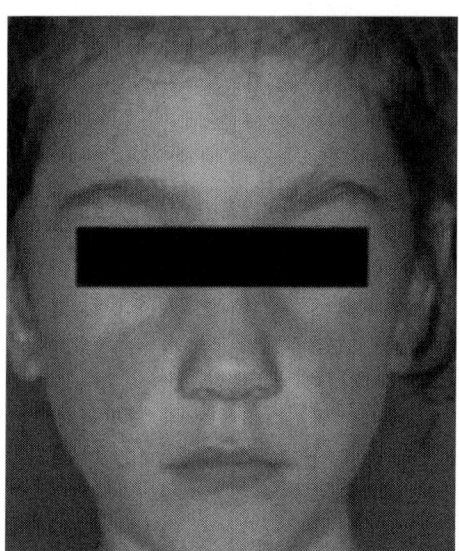

FIFTH DISEASE : ERYTHEMA INFECTIOSUM

Illness that has three distinct phases : In the first phase (2-4 days), bright-red erythema appears over the cheeks in a classic slapped-cheek appearance that spares the nasal, periorbital, and perioral regions. In the second phase (1-4 days), many eruption occurs on the extensor surfaces of the extremities. In the final stage (several days to weeks), the eruption fades.

Symptoms include fever, headache, and runny nose, followed by a pruritic rash on the face ("slapped cheek"), as well as the torso and extremities. The disease is self-limited.

The virus may also result in acute or persistent arthropathy, as well as so-called gloves-and-socks syndrome, characterized by purpuric eruptions on the hands and feet.

Treatment is generally supportive. Arthralgia may be treated with oral analgesics, those who suffer from pruritus may use antihistamines or topical antipruritic lotions.

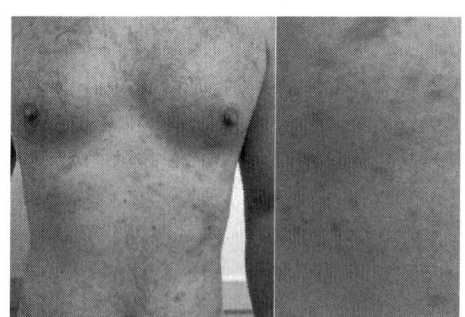

PITYRIASIS ROSEA

Salmon-coloured macule that enlarged over several days to become a patch with fine scales and a well-demarcated border. Over the next several weeks, a generalized bilateral, symmetrical macules oriented along body lines, with mild pruritus.

It begins as a solitary macule that is termed a "herald" or "mother" patch; after several days more lesions ("daughter" patches) appear on the torso and extremities.

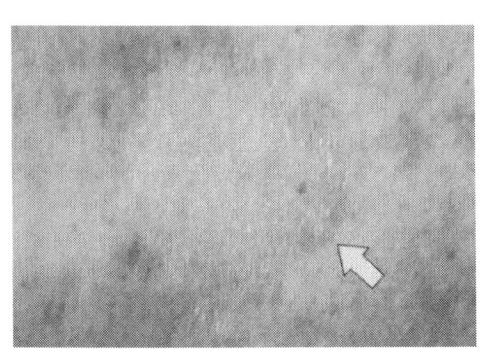	Treatment is largely symptomatic for relief of pruritus, with topical steroids and oral antihistamines used.
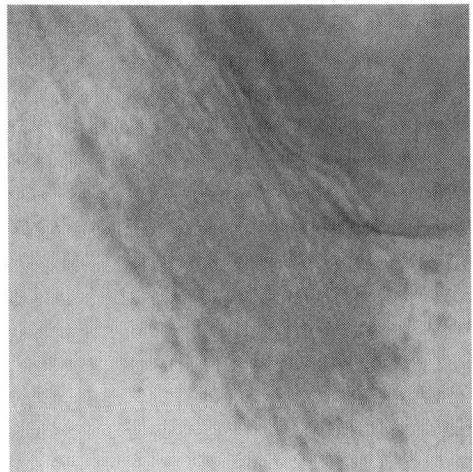	**INTERTRIGO** An inflammatory condition of skin folds, often from a candidal infection, but it also may be caused by bacteria, fungi, or viruses. Heat, moisture, friction, and lack of air circulation all provide ideal conditions for infection. It is most common in people who are diabetic or obese. Intertrigo is typically chronic with patients reporting itching, burning, and stinging of infected areas. Erythema, weeping, crusting, fissuring, pustules, or vesicles may all be present, depending on the duration of the inflammation. The diagnosis is usually clinical, but a skin scraping with KOH preparation may be used to rule out fungal infection. Treatment options include wound care, elimination of friction, heat, keeping the skin cool and dry; topical antifungals or antibiotics; low-dose topical steroids.

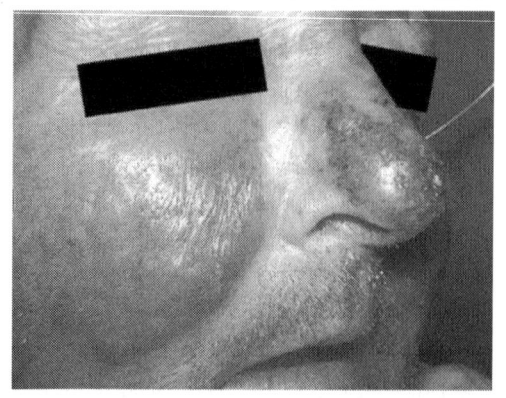

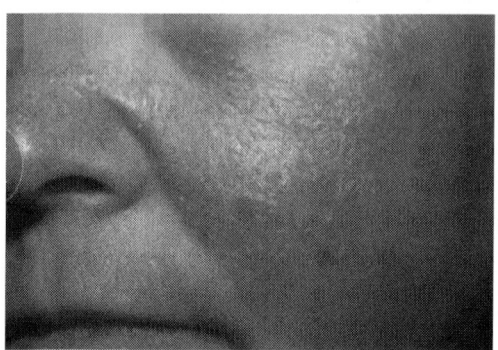

ERYSIPELAS

A cellulitis which is a small erythematous patch that progresses to a fiery, tense, and shiny plaque. The margins are well demarcated.

Treatment for 10-20 days with parenteral and/or oral antibiotics, typically penicillin (or a first generation cephalosporin or macrolide in penicillin allergic patients)

FOLLICULITIS

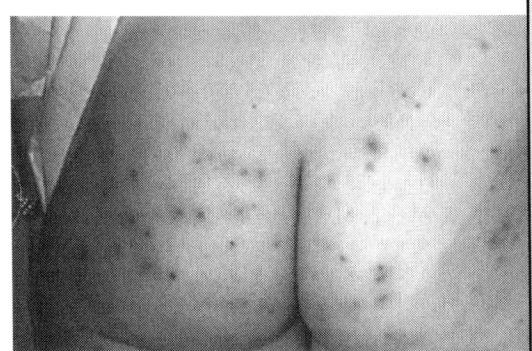

Caused by *Staph Aureus*, produces multiple small papules or pustules on an erythematous base, pierced by a central hair.

Different causes have been identified, including infection, trauma, friction, perspiration, and occlusion.

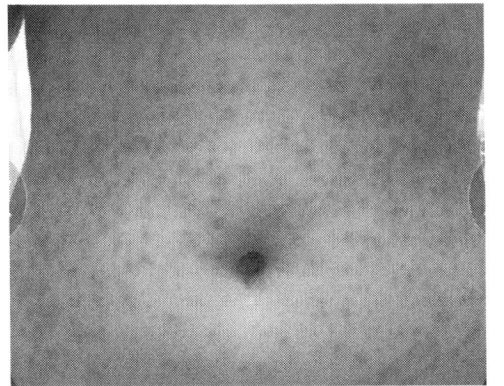

Folliculitis is typically self-limited and does not require treatment, but the use of antibacterial soaps is recommended for recurrent folliculitis.

Treatment of deep lesions or those that are resistant to therapy includes topical and/or oral antibiotics

I

Infective causes:

Pericarditis, endocarditis, costrochonditis, pneumonia

N

Neoplasm causes:

Lymphoma, Leukaemia, organ cancer

V

Vascular causes:

Ischaemic heart, Aneurysm, CCF, MI, PE, Angina, sickle cell

I

Inflammatory causes:

Rheumatic fever, Dressler syndrome, Anaphalaxis, Asthma

T

Traumatic causes:

Blunt, penetrating, chemical, fracture

E

Endocrine causes:

DKA, Carcinoid, pheochromocytoma

D

Degenerative causes:

Guillian barre

M

Metabolic causes:

Cystic fibrosis

D

Drugs/developmental causes:

Eissenmenger syndrome, statins

I

Infective causes:

Malaria, food poisoning, UTI, STI

N

Neoplasm causes:

Lymphoma, Leukaemia, organ cancer

V

Vascular causes:

Mesenteric ischaemia, AAA, RAS, MI

I

Inflammatory causes:

IBD, Coeliacs, Diverticulitis, appendicitis, endometriosis

T

Traumatic causes:

Blunt, penetrating, chemical

E

Endocrine causes:

DKA, Carcinoid, Hypercalcaemia

Degenerative causes:

Multiple sclerosis

D

M

Metabolic causes:

Liver disease, Renal disease, Cystic fibrosis

Drugs/developmental causes:

Torsion, hernia, NSAID, Opioid, Antibiotic

D

I

> Infective causes:
>
> Meningitis, Abscess, Congestion headache

N

> Neoplasm causes:
>
> Pituitary tumour, Leukaemia, organ cancer

V

> Vascular causes:
>
> Venous sinus thrombosis, SAH, AVM, aneurysm

I

> Inflammatory causes:
>
> Temporal arteritis, Cervicogenic headache

T

> Traumatic causes:
>
> Blunt, penetrating, chemical

E

> Endocrine causes:
>
> DKA, Conns, Hypercalcaemia, hyperthyroidism

D

> Degenerative causes:
>
> Multiple sclerosis

M

> Metabolic causes:
>
> Liver disease, renal disease

D

> Drugs/developmental causes:
>
> AVM

First identify any pre-existing risks such as:

- Premature baby
- Cardiac disease
- Genetic syndromes
- Diabetes
- Age

When taking a history make sure to clarify the number of:

1. Wet nappies
2. Episodes of diarrhoea
3. Episodes of Vomit
4. Duration of fever

3 minute Paediatric examination consists of:

- Exposing the torso
- Assessing respiratory rate and intercostal recession
- Palpate abdomen
- Assess pulse rate and hand temperature and saturation %
- Capillary refill and central capillary refill (forehead or torso)
- Listen to the back
- Finally, have a look in ears and throat and record their body temperature
- Run a blood glucose if concerned

With regards to body temperature a good rule is to remember 38 degrees or more in children 3 months or older and 39 degrees or more in children up 6 months or older.

<u>Difficulty in breathing</u>

Causes:

1.   Asthma
2.   Croup
3.   Bronchiolitis
4.   Pneumonia

With pneumonia in children the signs are very subtle therefore rely on the general signs of severe infection (lethargy, fever and a high heart rate, saturations). In children 3 years old high respiratory rate is enough to warrant a chest x-ray.

Red flags:

- Choking
- Apnoea – if previously the child became cyanosed or floppy
  Can be caused by respiratory infection, sepsis or meningitis.
- Severe asthma attack

<u>Fever</u>

Carry out the 3 minute paediatric examination.

Is there a high respiratory rate or heart rate?

Are there signs of peripheral shut down? (Test the capillary refill and feel the temperature of the hands and feet)

Duration of the fever?

How the child has behaved when the temperature is brought down with an antipyretic such as paracetamol or ibuprofen?

Has the child missed any routine vaccinations?

Red flags:

- Pneumonia
- UTI
- Joint infection
- Kawasaki disease
- Influenza
- Meningitis

Rashes

Often the reason for this is that parents and teachers know that a rash can be a sign of meningitis. Or it may be, that parents want to know if it is something specific e.g. measles or chickenpox.

Joint pains occur with a rash in several conditions, which include meningococcal septicaemia, Henoch Schonlein purpura, juvenile onset arthritis and leukaemia.

Accompanying symptoms may also include; a cough and sore eyes in measles or red eyes in Kawasaki disease, abdominal pain in Henoch-Schonlein Purpura, a recent burn in toxic shock syndrome, bleeding gums or nosebleeds and lethargy in leukaemia.

Abdominal pain

For acute problems, the top things you want to think about are urinary tract infection, and surgical causes. Normal appetite usually indicates the child is not suffering from a serious cause of abdominal pain. If the pain has kept the child awake, or awoken them from sleep, a serious diagnosis is more likely.

Surgical causes of abdominal pain include intussusception, bowel obstruction, appendicitis and rare things such as malrotation of the intestines, and Meckel's diverticulum

Also consider urinary tract infection, bowel obstruction, testicular torsion and appendicitis as these can sometimes present with only abdominal pain in children.

You don't need to know the exact diagnosis, but can usually pick up a child who needs an urgent operation by history and examination. The history will usually include not wanting to eat, quite severe pain, worse on movement, and vomiting. In particular if you hear of vomit with green bile in it, you must consider bowel obstruction.

Question 1.

What would a patient with Crohn's present with?

Question 2.

What complications can present in Crohn's?

Question 3.

List some causes of chronic liver disease (CLD)?

Question 4.

What blood tests are used to assess liver function?

Question 5.

In septic arthritis what investigations should you do?

Question 6.

What are the red flag symptoms of lower back pain?

Question 7.

What drugs may a patient in urinary retention have been on?

Question 8.

What are the treatment options for prostatic hyperplasia?

Question 9.

How do you investigate acute urinary retention?

Question 10.

What are causes of glomerular nephritis?

Question 11.

List three categories of causes of AKI

Question 12.

List four types of drugs which are nephrotoxic

Question 13.

What is the difference between transudate and exudate pleural effusions?

Question 14.

Name some causes of transudative pleural effusions?

Question 15.

Name some causes of exudative pleural effusions?

Question 16.

What is are sepsis six?

Question 17.

What is an extracapsular neck of femur fracture?

Question 18.

What is specific about the pain of compartment syndrome?

Question 19.

What are the causes of peptic ulcer disease?

Question 20.

What liver related causes are there for jaundice?

Question 21.
What could cause acute delirium?

Question 22.
What are the causes of fibrosis?

Question 23.
List the clinical features of asthma

Question 24.
What is the main concern on an ABG in acute asthma?

Question 25.
What dose of adrenaline would you give to a patient with anaphylaxis?

Question 26.
What is the ratio of compressions to breaths during CPR?

Question 27.
List are the reversible causes of a cardiac arrest

Question 1:

- Diarrhoea (can be bloody and/or chronic)
- Abdominal pain
- Weight loss
- Mouth ulcers

Question 2:

- Bowel thickened and narrowed.

- Deep fissures and ulcers in mucosa.

- Fistulae, abscesses and strictures.

Question 3:

- Alcohol

- Viral

- NAFLD

- Due to diabetes, metabolic syndrome
- DM2, Hypertension, Obesity, Hyperlipidaemia

Question 4

- PT (prothrombin time [or INR, which is derived from PT]), platelets and albumin

Question 5

- Bloods (especially for WCC, CRP and ESR)
- Blood cultures
- Aspirate joint and
  - Send the fluid for urgent microscopy, culture and start antibiotics.

Question 6

- Age <20 or >55

- Current or recent infection (especially TB, but staph and others will infect the spine)

- Immunosuppression (infection)

- Abdominal mass (malignancy)

- Tricyclic medication
- Anti-muscarinic medication
- Opiates
- Anti-histamines

o Alpha blockers such as Tamsulosin, 5-alpha reductase inhibitors e.g. finasteride

Surgical

o Transurethral resection of prostate (TURP), transurethral incision of prostate (TUIP)

Catheterise

o Post-catheter: Measure residual volume of bladder in first 10-15 minutes

o Residual volumes of greater than one litre make patients more likely to fail a trial without catheter (TWOC) and increase the chances of have recurrent retention

- Autoimmune nephropathy and sclerosis of glomerulosa segments

o Pre-renal

o Intrinsic renal

o Post-renal

o ACEIs

o ARBs

o NSAIDs

o Aminoglycosides e.g. gentamicin

Transudate

o   Protein <30 g/l

Exudate

o   Protein >30 g/l

Failures

o   Left ventricular failure

o   Liver failure (cirrhotic liver disease)

Pulmonary

o   Pulmonary embolism (can be transudates or exudates)

o   Malignancy (5% are transudate)

- Infection
- Malignancy
- Rheumatological
- Pulmonary embolism (can be transudates or exudates)

- Oxygen titrated to achieve S_pO_2 94-98% or 88-92% if known to have COPD
- Check lactate
- Take blood cultures
- Give IV antibiotics
- Commence IV fluid resuscitation
- Monitor urine output

- These are fractures of the neck of the femur which occur outside the capsule of the hip joint

- It is typically out of proportion

- H. Pylori
- NSAIDs
- Steroids
- Smoking
- Alcohol
- Stress

- Cirrhosis
- Malignancy
- Viral hepatitis
- Drugs

- Infection
- Pain
- Constipation
- Urinary retention
- Drugs

Upper lobe

o   TB

o   Ankylosing spondylosis

o   Sarcoid

o   Pneumoconiosis

Lower

o   Bronchiectasis

o   Rheumatoid Arthritis

o   Drugs

- Cough
- Dyspnoea
- Wheeze
- Chest tightness

Question 24

- Low pH
- >PaCO2
- <PaO2

Question 25

- 500 micrograms (0.5 ml of 1:1,000) IM

Question 26

- 30 chest compressions to 2 breaths (30:2)

Question 27

The reversible causes are remembered by the "4 Hs and 4 Ts"

○ Hypoxia: ensure a patent airway and give high flow oxygen

○ Hypovolaemia: commence IV fluid resuscitation

○ Hypo/hyperkalaemia and other metabolic derangements: check the VBG for any metabolic derangements and correct accordingly. Look at previous bloods for likely magnesium concentrations or correct empirically.

○ Hypothermia: check the patient's temperature and if low re-warm to 32-34 °C

○ Tension pneumothorax: auscultate the patient's lung fields during ventilations and perform needle decompression if required

○ Tamponade (cardiac): obtain a beside echocardiogram (echo) and perform pericardiocentesis as indicated

○ Toxins: check the patient's drug chart and/or enquire about recent medications or overdoses in the collateral history

○ Thrombosis (pulmonary or cardiac): obtain a bedside ultrasound and identify symptoms and risk factors in the collateral history

Questions 1.

A 61-year old male with a diagnosis of lung cancer presents with increasing tiredness and dizziness. Investigations show the following:

Plasma sodium concentration:	125mmol/L (137-144)
Potassium:	3.5mmol/L (3.5-4.9)
Urea:	4.2 mmol/L (2.5-7.5)
Creatinine:	70 µmol/L (60-110)

Which is the likely cause?

A.   Addison's disease
B.   Diabetes insipidus
C.   Hypoadrenalism due to adrenal metastases
D.   Malignant nephrotic syndrome
E.   Syndrome of inappropriate ADH secretion

Question 2.

The following result is from a 57-year old male who is admitted with acute onset of chest pain:

Serum   Cholesterol: 8.3 mmol/L (<5.2)

He has a strong family history of ischaemic heart disease. Where might you expect to find abnormalities upon examination of this man?

A.   Ejection systolic murmur
B.   Heberden's nodes
C.   Hepatomegaly
D.   Splinter haemorrhages in nail beds
E.   Tendon nodules

Question 3.

The T wave in the ECG is caused by which of the following mechanisms?

A.   A slow transmission through the A-V node and junctional fibres
B.   Atrial depolarization
C.   Atrial repolarization
D.   Ventricular depolarization
E.   Ventricular repolarization

A 73-year old man has become aware of his heart beating irregularly. On examination his pulse appears irregularly irregular with a rate of 56 bpm. What would you expect to see on ECG?

A. A P wave preceding each QRS complex
B. Bifid P waves
C. No P wave preceding each QRS complex
D. Regular P waves but not associated with QRS complexes
E. Small P waves

Question 5.

Mr Echol, a 50-year old man, visits his GP surgery to review his blood pressure since he has DM2. It shows 149/122 mmHg. His heart rate is 82 bpm, he smokes 20 cigarettes a day, and has a diet rich in alcohol and saturated fats. What is your initial step in treating this man's hypertension?

A. Lifestyle advice and review
B. Prescribe bendroflumethiazide
C. Prescribe furosemide
D. Prescribe lisinopril
E. Prescribe mannitol

Question 6.

Hane, a 34-year old man presents to A&E at 1am after taking an unplanned overdose of 15 paracetamol tablets with vodka. This is his 5th attendance to A&E. He reports taking the tablets at 10pm. What is your immediate steps?

A. Immediate blood paracetamol levels and psych review
B. Immediate prescription of Parvolex IVI and delayed blood paracetamol levels
C. Immediate psych review and delayed blood paracetamol levels
D. Immediate LFTs and blood alcohol levels
E. No immediate action required for this level of ingestion

179

Question 7.

During a more detailed review of his background he has had multiple intensive relationships but they do not seem to last. He describes himself as 'hollow', and has felt this way for many months. What is the most likely diagnosis?

    A.   Anankastic personality disorder
    B.   Depressive episode
    C.   Emotionally unstable personality disorder –borderline type
    D.   Emotionally unstable personality disorder –impulsive type
    E.   Histrionic personality disorder

Question 8.

A man with paranoid schizophrenia is admitted following a relapse in his psychotic symptoms. On admission he is described as repeating the words the nurses say to him. What phenomenon is this?

    A.   Echolalia
    B.   Logorrhea
    C.   Paragrammatism
    D.   Paraphasia
    E.   Verbigeration

Question 9.

An elderly lady is admitted to the acute psychiatric ward. She has stopped eating and drinking because she believes her stomach and organs are rotten. She is depressed and denies hearing voices. What is the description of her delusions?

    A.   Delusions of control
    B.   Delusions of guilt
    C.   Delusions of reference
    D.   Hypochondriacal delusions
    E.   Nihilistic delusions

Question 10.

A 50-year old man presents with a two month history of weight loss and sweats. Which of the following is the most appropriation blood test?

    A.   Blood cultures
    B.   ESR
    C.   Full blood count
    D.   Liver function tests
    E.   Thyroid   function tests

Question 11.

A 35-year old man is brought after ingesting 70 tablets of amitriptyline 50mg. He is tachycardic but has a normal ECG and is becoming drowsy. What is the antidote for amitriptyline poisoning?

A.   Sodium   bicarbonate
B.   Doxazosin
C.   Flumazenil
D.   Atropine
E.   Glucagon

Question 12.

A 55-year old man presents with increasing tiredness. He was diagnosed with a bronchial carcinoma. His electrolytes reveal:

Sodium   108 mmol/L (137-144)

Potassium   3.6 mmol/L   (3.5-4.9)

Urea   3.2 mmol/L   (2.5-7.5)

Creatinine   67 μmol/L   (60-110)

What is the most appropriate investigation for this patient?

A.   CT chest and abdomen
B.   Serum ADH concentration
C.   Short Synacthen test
D.   Thyroid   function tests
E.   Urine osmolality and sodium concentration

Question 13.

This man presents with sweating and headaches.

How would you confirm the diagnosis?

A.   Alkaline   phosphatase
B.   Glucose   concentration
C.   Oral glucose tolerance test
D.   Short Synacthen test
E.   Skull x-ray

This woman presents with weight gain, weakness and fatigue.

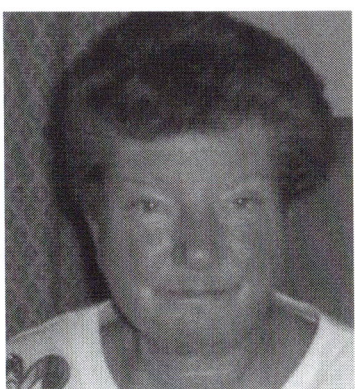

Which of the following is the most likely diagnosis?

A. Acne rosacea
B. Carcinoid syndrome
C. Cushing's syndrome
D. Mitral stenosis
E. Systemic lupus erythematosus

Question 15.

Which one of the following is associated with Cushing's syndrome?

A. Colonic   neoplasia
B. Diabetes insipidus
C. Diabetes mellitus
D. Renal artery stenosis
E. Thrombophilia

Question 16.

This patient present with headache and sweating which has gotten worse over the years. He is very tall and has a broad jaw and large skull. Which of the following would you expect to find on examination of the eyes?

A. Bitemporal hemianopia
B. Central   scotoma
C. Homonymous hemianopia
D. Papilloedema
E. Ptosis

A 23-year old female with a six month history of amenorrhoea and galactorrhoea. She takes no medications. A pregnancy test is negative.

Which investigations would be most appropriate?

A. LH/FSH   concentration
B. MRI pituitary
C. Oestradiol concentration
D. Prolactin concentration
E. Thyroid   function test

Question 18

A 60-year old female with DM2 is referred for feeling unwell and has poor glycaemic control with glucose readings of 25 mmol/L. His U&E's are:

Serum	sodium	138 mmol/L	(137-144)
Serum	potassium	5.8 mmol/L	(3.5-4.9)
Serum	urea	20 mmol/L	(2.5-7.5)
Serum	creatinine	350 μmol/L	(60-110)

She has a temperature of 39C, heart rate of 108 bpm, blood pressure of 96/60mmHg, and respiration rate of 32/minute. The urine dip is positive for blood and protein.

What is the most likely diagnosis?

A. Diabetic ketoacidosis
B. Hyperosmolar non-ketotic state
C. Lactic acidosis
D. Sepsis
E. Type 4 renal tubular acidosis

Question 19.

A man is treated with morphine, aspirin, clopidgrel, enoxaparin and metolprolol. He has ust developed worsening of chest pain and his heart rate has dropped to 33 bpm. His BP is 135/75 mmHg. An ECG demonstrates complete heart block. What has precipitated this?

A. Anterior myocardial infarction
B. Beta blocker overdose
C. Inferior myocardial infarction
D. Morphine overdose
E. Posterior myocardial infarction

A 32-year old asthmatic has presented with 24hr history of worsening wheeze. The patient is short of breath despite 3 sets of salbutamol nebulisers. There is reduced air entry and resonant percussion in the left lung with a trachea deviated to the right. What is the most likely diagnosis?

A. Panic attack
B. Pneumonia
C. Pulmonary embolism
D. Simple pneumothorax
E. Tension pneumothorax

Question 21.

A 40-year old woman is admitted to MAU with 36 hours of fever and a sore throat. The breathing is noisy and high pitched. She has a temperature of 39.4 C and raised heart rate and respiratory rate. What is the most likely diagnosis?

A. Anaphylaxis
B. Bacterial tracheitis
C. Croup
D. Foreign body aspiration
E. Laryngospasm

Question 22.

A 74 year old lady had a severe headache, nausea, vomiting and sensitivity to light. On examination she had neck stiffness and foot extension on plantar reflex. Lumbar puncture shows blood in the CSF. What was the most likely diagnosis?

A. Glioblastoma
B. Ruptured berry aneurysm
C. Meningitis
D. Bleeding into a medulloblastoma
E. Head injury causing subdural haemorrhage

A 20-year-old Caribbean man is seen with severe pain present across his body, most severe abdominally. He says he is usually given morphine for pain relief. What is the most likely diagnosis?

    A.   Drug seeking
    B.   Haemoglobin Bart's
    C.   Ischaemic gut
    D.   Sickle cell crisis
    E.   Thalassaemia

Question 24.

A 67-year-old man presents to you with severe abdominal pain. The pain originally started in his left loin and radiates to the groin. He also complains of pain radiating to his back. Observations reveal a temperature of 37.3°C, oxygen saturation 94% on air, blood pressure of 80/50 mmHg and a heart rate of 134 beats per minute. He also has a 40 pack per year history of smoking. What is the most likely diagnosis?

    A.   Acute appendicitis
    B.   Diverticulitis
    C.   Leaking abdominal aortic aneurysm
    D.   Peritonitis
    E.   Renal calculi

Question 25.

A 85-year-old male presents with abdominal pain. He gives a past history of stroke and myocardial infarction. On examination the stools were maroon coloured. Lactate is 6 mmol/L (normal <2.2 mmol/L). Which is the most likely diagnosis?

    A.   Acute gastric bleed
    B.   Acute mesenteric ischaemia
    C.   Crohn's disease
    D.   Ulcerative colitis
    E.   Diverticulitis

Question 26.

A 45-year-old man presents having woken up with a painful left foot. He is worried because he cannot feel his foot or move his toes. On examination, the foot is very pale and cold to touch. What is the most likely diagnosis?

A. Acute limb ischaemia
B. Compartment syndrome
C. Gangrene
D. Intermittent claudication
E. Stroke

1 2 3 4 5 6 7 8 9 10 11 12 13 14 15 16 17 18 19 20 21 22 23 24 25 26
Answers: E, E, E, C, A, C, C, A, E, E, A, E, C, C, C, A, D, D, C, E, B, B, D, C, B, A.

186

Question 1

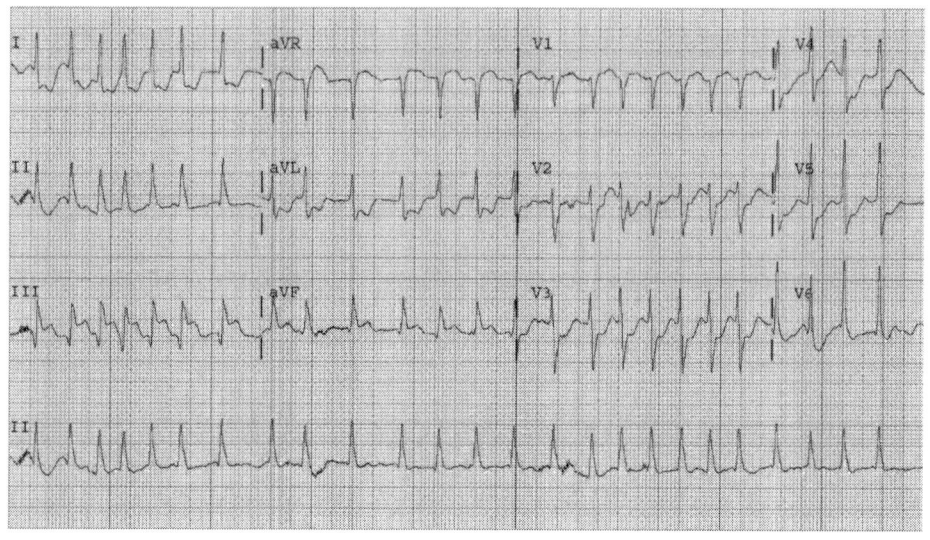

Answer:

Rate: 110/150

Rhythm: Irregularly irregular

This ECG shows atrial fibrillation (AF) with a fast ventricular response.

Question 2

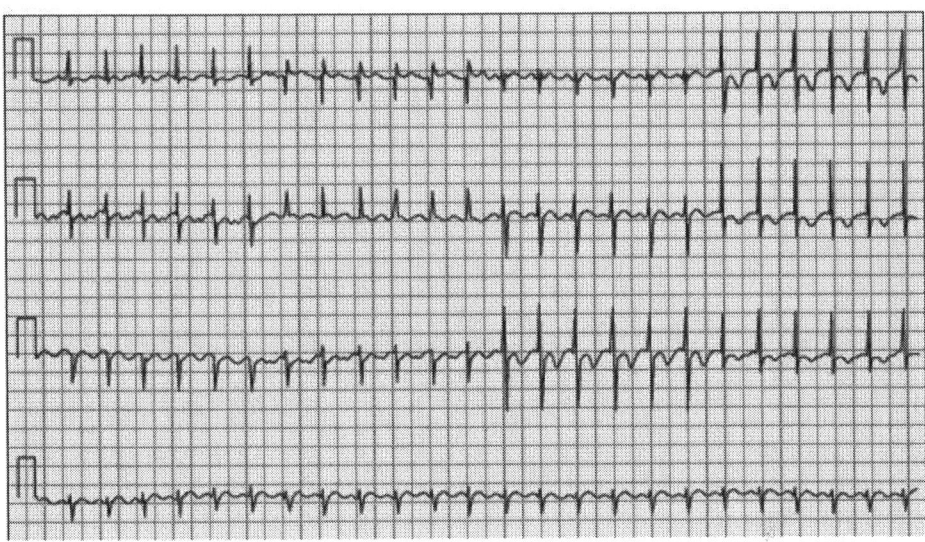

Answer:

Rate: 150

Rhythm : Regular

This is atrial flutter. The atria contracts extremely fast causing a 'seesaw' appearance.

Question 3

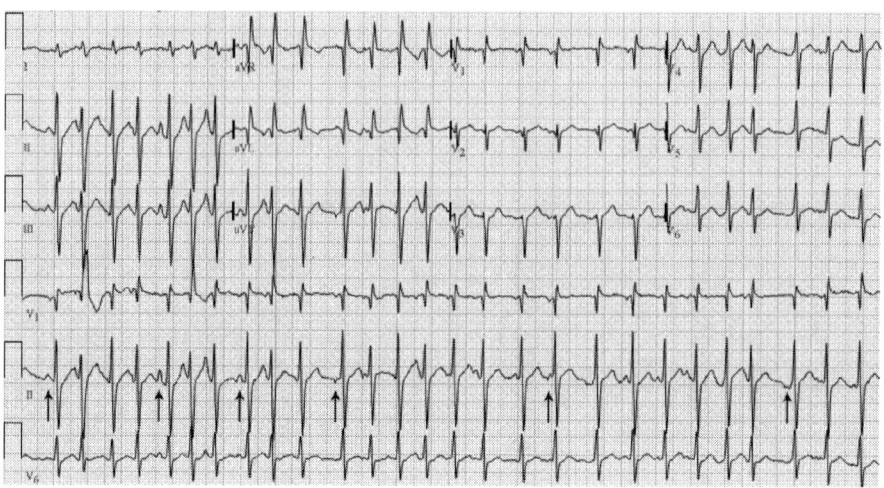

Answer:

Rate: 120/150

Rhythm: Irregularly irregular

This is polymorphic atrial tachycardia. It occurs in respiratory disease.

Question 4

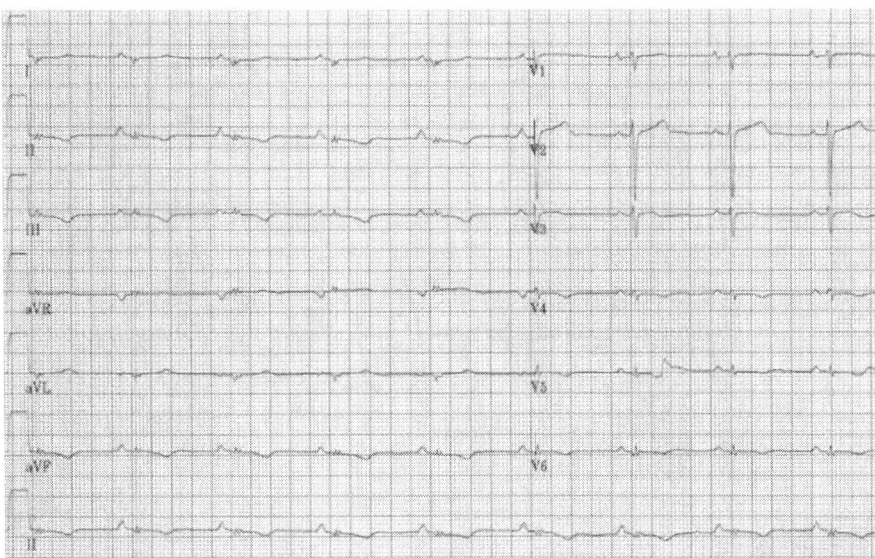

Answer:

This is pulseless electrical activity (PEA). This patient is in cardiac arrest and needs chest compressions and advanced life support.

Question 5

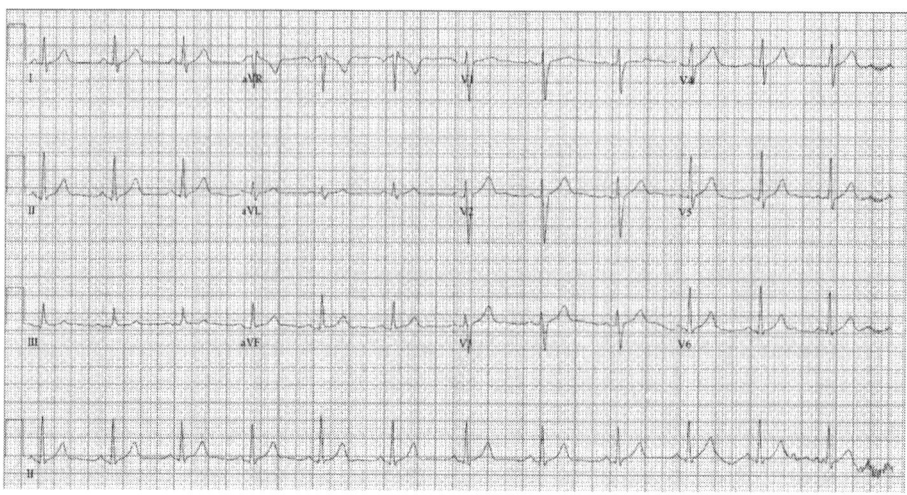

Answer:

Rate: 90

Rhythm: Regular

This is a normal ECG.

Question 6

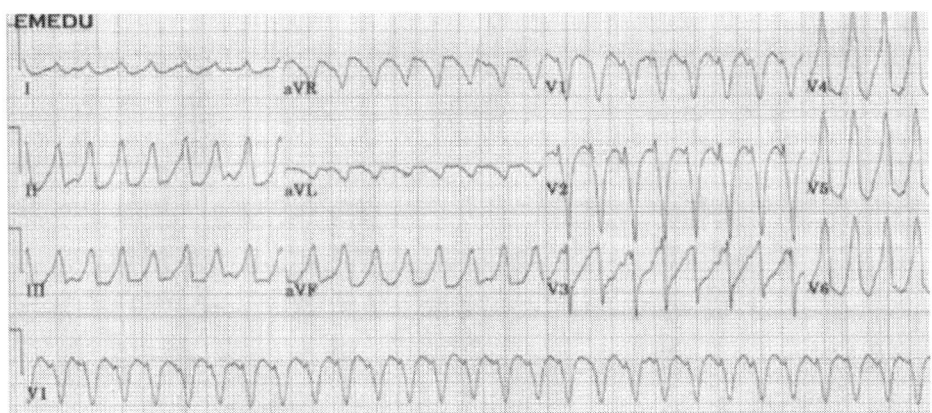

Answer:

Rate: 180

Rhythm: Regular

This is ventricular tachycardia (VT) and the patient would have no central pulse. He should be treated with chest compressions immediately. This is a shockable rhythm.

Question 7

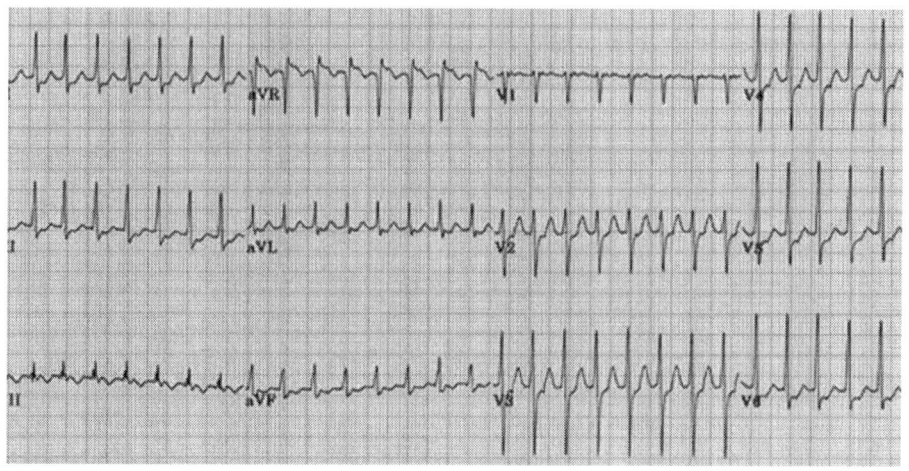

Answer:

Rate: 200

Rhythm: Regular

This is a supraventricular tachycardia (SVT). Treatment includes vagal manoeuvres followed by adenosine.

Question 8

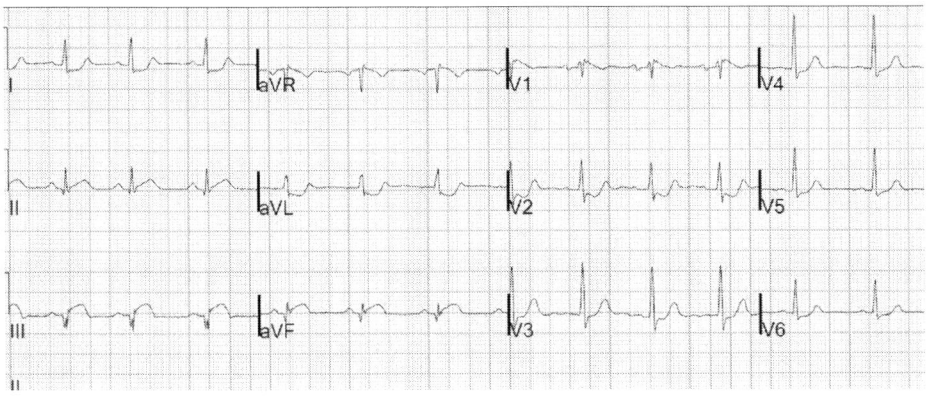

Answer:

Rate: 100

Rhythm: Regular

This is ECG shows an inferior STEMI because of ST elevation in leads 2,3 and AVF

Question 9

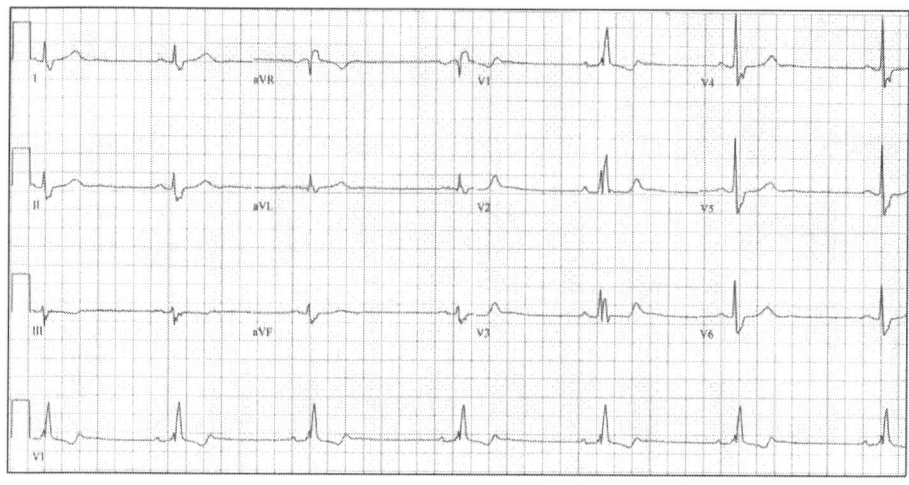

Answer:

Rate: 40 bpm

Rhythm : Regular

This is sinus bradycardia. Tests including thyroid function, x-ray, echocardiogram and 24-hour tape are first-line investigations.

Question 10

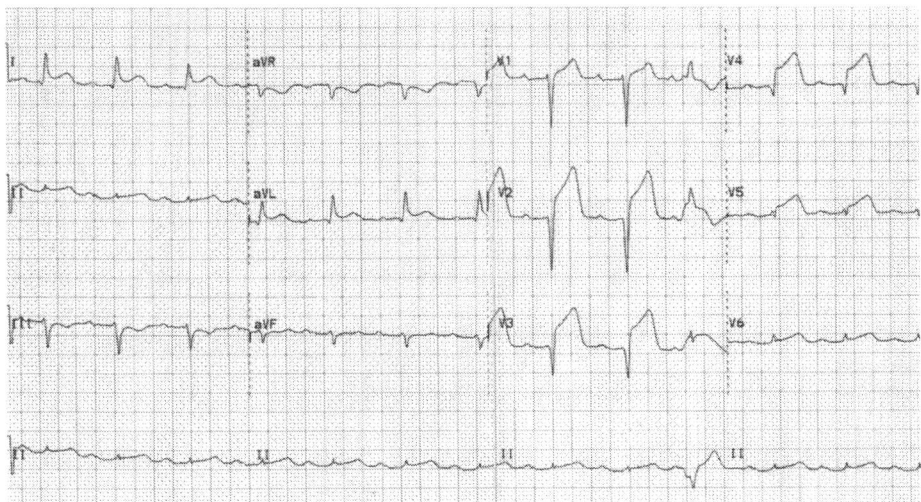

Answer:

Rate: 80

Rhythm: Regular

Grossly elevated in V2, V3, and V4

This patient should be assessed and treated urgently for a STEMI with primary coronary intervention (PCI). This would be a time for CAN I/ME SOB management also.

Question 11

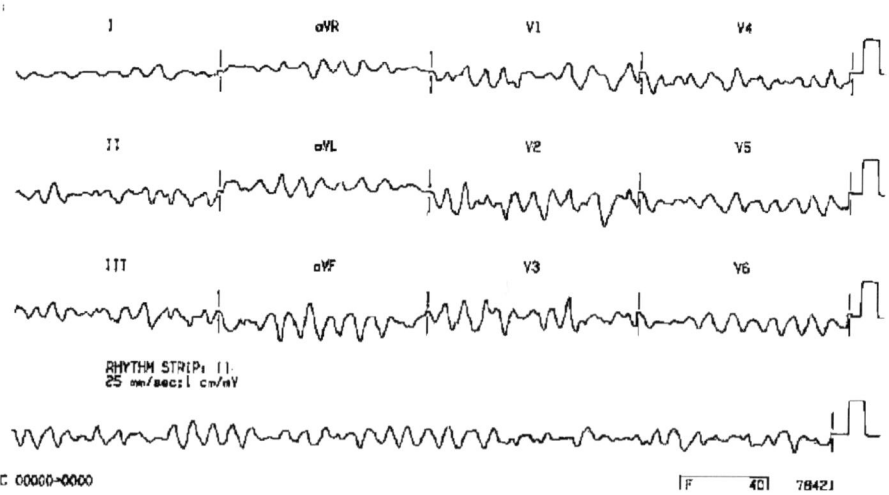

Answer:

Rhythm : Irregular

This is the classic ECG pattern of fibrillation (VF).

Question 12

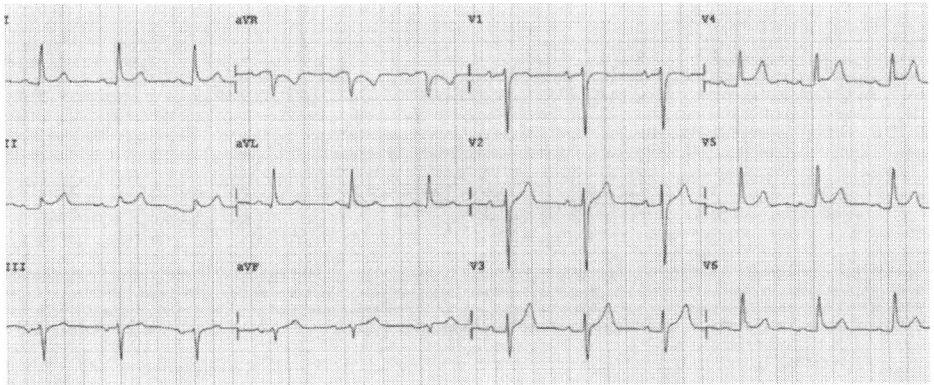

Answer:

Rate: 60

Rhythm: Regular

Widespread ST elevation (saddle shaped)

Pericarditis often presents in young people after a viral illness. Notice the widespread saddle-shaped ST elevation and PR depression.

Question 13

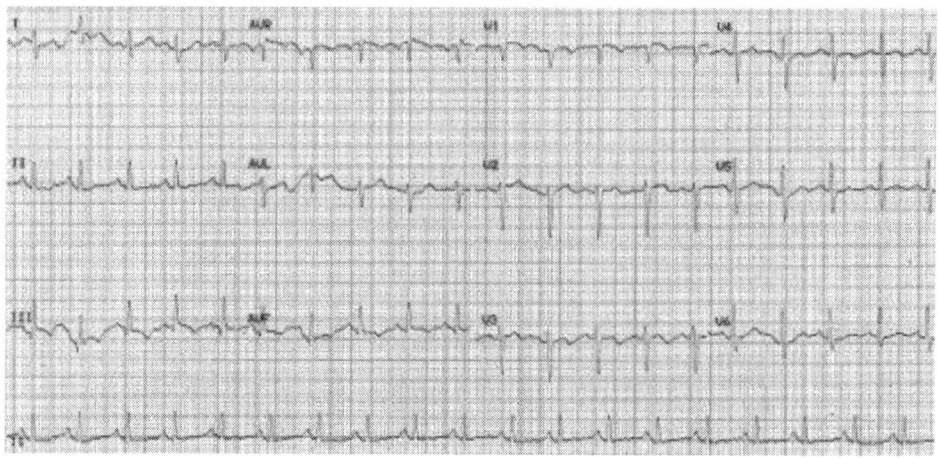

Answer:

Rate: 100

Rhythm: Regular

In PE the ECG findings of 'S1Q3T3' although this is very rare and it usually presents as a sinus tachycardia.

Question 14

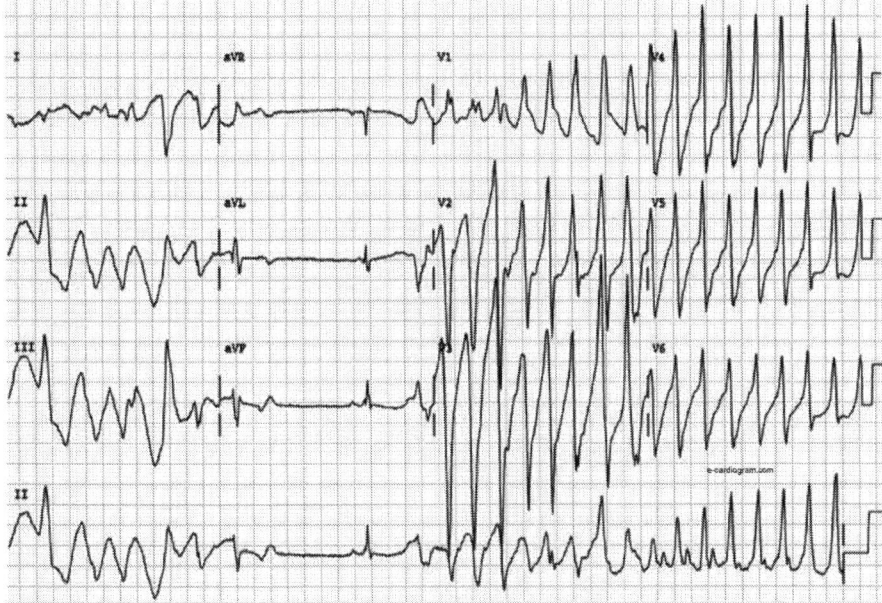

Answer:

Rate: variable

Rhythm : Irregular

This ECG shows polymorphic VT or Torsade's de pointes (twisting of the points). Causes include medications and electrolyte imbalance.

Question 1.

pH: 7.50 (7.35-7.45)

pO2: 7.4 (10–14)

pCO2: 3.8 (4.5–6.0)

HCO3: 22 (22-26)

BE: -1 (-2 to +2)

What's the diagnosis?

This is type 1 respiratory failure.

Question 2.

pH: 7.37 (7.35-7.45)

pO2: 8.1 (10–14)

pCO2: 7.7 (4.5–6.0)

HCO3: 31 (22-26)

BE: +5 (-2 to +2)

What's the diagnosis?

This is a compensated respiratory acidosis.

Question 3.

pH: 7.21 (7.35-7.45)

pO2: 7.3 (10–14)

pCO2: 8.5 (4.5–6.0)

HCO3: 30 (22-26)

BE: +4 (-2 to +2)

What's the diagnosis?

This is Type 2 respiratory failure

Question 4.

pH: 7.49 (7.35-7.45)

pO2: 12.0 (10–14)

pCO2: 3.6 (4.5–6.0)

HCO3: 22 (22-26)

BE: +2 (-2 to +2)

Other values within normal range

What's the diagnosis?

This is a respiratory alkalosis

Question 5.

pH: 7.23 (7.35-7.45)

pO2: 11.5 (10–14)

pCO2: 3.0 (4.5–6.0)

HCO3: 11 (22-26)

BE: -15 (-2 to +2)

Potassium: 4.5

Sodium: 135

Chloride: 100

What's the diagnosis?

Metabolic acidosis.

Question 6.

pH: 7.59 (7.35-7.45)

pO2: 10.8 (10–14)

pCO2: 5.2 (4.5–6.0)

HCO3: 34 (22-26)

BE: +5 (-2 to +2)

What's the diagnosis?

This is metabolic alkalosis

Question 7.

pH: 7.10 (7.35-7.45)

pO2: 12.0 (10–14)

pCO2: 3.2 (4.5–6.0)

HCO3: 10 (22-26)

BE: -18 (-2 to +2)

What's the diagnosis?

Metabolic acidosis

Question 8.

pH: 7.13 (7.35-7.45)

pO2: 11.8 (10–14)

pCO2: 3.0 (4.5–6.0)

HCO3: 9 (22-26)

BE: -17 (-2 to +2)

Glucose: 22

What's the diagnosis?

This is diabetic ketoacidosis (DKA).

Question 9.

pH: 7.21 (7.35-7.45)

pO2: 9.0 (10–14)

pCO2: 6.4 (4.5–6.0)

HCO3: 16 (22-26)

BE: -8 (-2 to +2)

What's the diagnosis?

This is a mixed respiratory and metabolic acidosis.

Printed in Great Britain
by Amazon